From The Nursery End

FROM THE NURSERY END

Cricket's 18 Top Coaches
Reveal How Players Are Made

Brian Radford

Arthur Barker Limited London

A SUBSIDIARY OF WEIDENFELD (PUBLISHERS) LIMITED

Published in Great Britain by
Arthur Barker Limited
91 Clapham High Street
London SW4 7TA

ISBN 0 213 16916 9

Printed in Great Britain by
Butler and Tanner Limited,
Frome and London

Contents

To Toby,
who lives for the game.

Preface

With very little exception, England's eighteen top coaches are the men on whom our best cricketers, county clubs and eventually our international cricketing image depend. It is they who discover the talent, shape, bully, cajole and polish it up and make it presentable for the public. They are the star-makers. The professionals behind the professionals. A group of backroom men who rarely are given the praise and gratitude that they deserve.

It is significant that every one of them has played county cricket at some time in his professional life. They know the requirements. A number, indeed, have represented England all over the world. They speak with experience, vision and a fervent desire to produce the best. Above all they are realistic, frank and fearless in their comments.

The coaches speak as candidly about their colleagues as they do about their opponents. They tell of the brilliant West Indian batsman who was so bad at sixteen that the county of his choice turned him down twice as an abysmal failure. He couldn't bat, couldn't catch and couldn't throw. Now he is about the best in the world in all three departments. They describe the England wicketkeeper who blew his chance because he was too lazy. Also the ambitious batsman who trained so hard the coach thought he had cancer. As well as the cheats and jokers, the tough and the weak.

No punches are pulled. Why should they be? Without the coaches any number of county players would still be collecting their runs and wickets in obscure leagues on village greens.

For their conviviality and willingness to talk so openly, I thank them all. Their dedication and expertise are a credit to our game.

The Coaches

Derbyshire	*Philip Russell*
Essex	*Ray East*
Glamorgan	*Kevin Lyons*
Gloucestershire	*Graham Wiltshire*
Hampshire	*Peter Sainsbury*
Kent	*Colin Page*
Lancashire	*John Savage*
Leicestershire	*Ken Higgs*
Middlesex	*Don Bennett*
Northamptonshire	*Brian Reynolds*
Nottinghamshire	*Ken Taylor (also manager)*
Somerset	*Peter Robinson*
Surrey	*David Gibson*
Sussex	*Stewart Storey*
Warwickshire	*Alan Oakman*
Worcestershire	*Basil d'Oliveira*
Yorkshire	*Doug Padgett*
Lord's Indoor School	*Don Wilson and Gordon Jenkins*

1

Players, young and old

A stocky, confident West Indian walked out to take guard in the nets at Hampshire's indoor school. Highly recommended as a certainty for stardom, the sixteen-year-old lad crouched low to face his first delivery. Peter Sainsbury, that wily left-arm spinner who harvested a colossal 1,058 wickets in his 22-year career, moved in to bowl. The batsman groped forward, failed to connect, and the ball flew over the stumps. Sainsbury smiled. And ran up again . . . and again. Each time the lad looked mesmerised. Hopelessly out of touch and quite often out of his depth.

As the session ended, the tortured young batsman took off his pads, and Sainsbury stood alongside him. Sympathetic as usual, he said, 'Now look here, young Greenidge, why don't you go back to Reading, think hard, work hard, and perhaps one day we can give you another chance.'

So Gordon Greenidge went home . . . and a week later Hampshire received yet another call from Reading's ecstatic match secretary.

Peter Sainsbury: Gordon had gone back and scored yet another hundred. I couldn't believe it. So I said he could come down again. I agreed to take a second look. But he was no better. He was useless. If I had been county coach then, I would have told him to go away and forget about cricket.

Leo Harrison and I bowled to him and he couldn't hit the ball. It didn't matter whether it was fast, medium or slow. And he couldn't catch. And he couldn't field. Yet it never seemed to worry him. He had a marvellous temperament for someone so young. Then, when he left us and went back to play in his own environment, he would hit hundred after hundred.

He was the worst fielder I had seen. He couldn't run, couldn't throw, and his catching was appalling. He would pick up the ball and instead of throwing it over the stumps, he would sling it, like a stone, between mid-wicket and mid-on.

Then one evening everything changed in a single shot. I remember it like yesterday. Gordon was in the nets and I bowled him a beauty. The ball pitched about middle-and-leg, and on a perfect length. It was a good delivery. But all I saw was a blurr. His feet moved like I'd never seen feet move before. His arms flashed, and his whole body suddenly sprung into action. Everything was lightning fast. The bat came down in a perfect arc and at great speed, and the ball rocketed into the net on the leg side.

'Good God,' I thought. 'This kid really can bat!'

From that shot to today Gordon has never looked back. Now he rates as the finest opening batsman in the world, and his close fielding, ground fielding and throwing are just about perfect.

So yet again the danger of selecting and rejecting players on first impressions was hammered home to me. Without that second chance, Gordon might still be slamming century after century for Reading and working in a local factory. His unique brilliance would have been lost to cricket lovers all over the world.

Gifted with that imperturbable temperament, Greenidge matured fast. Soon he was forming one of the most formidable opening partnerships in county cricket history.

With the immaculate Barry Richards at one end, and the dynamic Greenidge at the other, opening bowlers found themselves hammered to every corner of the ground.

In both style and technique they were far apart, but in scoring runs they were equally devastating.

Sainsbury recalls the arrival of Richards at Hampshire:

I remember clearly the day he came in. I had the traumatic experience of bowling to him in the nets. What I noticed about him straightaway was his superb balance. He had come to Britain with a Young South African side. Mike Procter was also with them.

Many times I have seen the very best batsmen struggling against good bowlers, but not Barry. He struck everything in the middle of the bat. He never moved an eyelid, let alone a foot, before a ball was bowled at him, no matter how fast it came. He was extra-special. He was the type of player everyone in the dressing-room went outside to see. No one went for a pee, lit a cigarette, or even read *The Sporting Life* when Barry was batting. They just watched, in case they missed something they would never see again.

His cover-drive was sheer poetry and perfection. People have asked me if he had a flaw. Well, if he did, it was that he got bored after scoring a hundred. That's when he became vulnerable.

He was different from Gordon. Barry relied on timing. You'd hardly see his arms move. But when Gordon hit a four or a six, you'd see every muscle ripple.

In his position as chief coach, Peter Sainsbury was largely responsible for the signing of Chris Smith, ironically another brilliant South African to open with Greenidge.

Towards the end of the 1984 season, Hampshire appointed Mark Nicholas as their new captain, an erudite all-rounder who came to the club's notice when John Harvey, resident coach at Bradfield College, telephoned Sainsbury and suggested that he should look at this free-scoring student. Remembering Harvey from his Derbyshire days, Sainsbury knew him as a good judge and immediately invited Nicholas for a trial in the Hampshire second team.

Peter Sainsbury: Mark had a dream start. He hit a hundred in that first match and everything grew from there.

Many good judges felt that Nicholas should have been brought in to bolster England's batting in the 1984 débâcle against the West Indies, but Sainsbury says:

I'm glad they didn't pick him. And that goes for Chris Smith, too. Both have a lot to offer, but going in against the West Indies could have destroyed them at this stage in their career. They could cope with the Pakistanis, Indians and New Zealanders, but the West Indians are a bit special. Compared with other countries it's cannons versus bows and arrows.

Chris, of course, had already played for England, but I think the selectors were right to leave him out this time. By his standards he had a bad start to the 1984 season, and it was strange that he actually came back to form in a match for which he wasn't even picked.

David Turner's wife was suddenly taken ill and David came and asked to be released. It was so late in the morning that the team sheet had already been passed to our opponents Leicestershire and we had to ask their captain Peter Willey for permission to bring Chris in.

Chris scored 95 on the Sunday, 25 on the Monday and 75 on the Tuesday. And that was against Andy Roberts and Jonathan Agnew, two of the quickest bowlers in the game.

Some people have said that Chris doesn't play the real quickies very well, but he's never given me that impression.

Obviously we talked about his loss of form, and to be honest the only difference in his play in 1984 from 1983 was that he was getting out in the twenties and thirties whereas the previous year he had been going on to make hundreds.

With Gordon Greenidge on West Indian duty in 1984, it ironically opened the way for Paul Terry to put his skills in the shop window and he did so well with several centuries in June, that England called him up to oppose Greenidge and his Caribbean colleagues, with disastrous consequences.

After scoring just eight and one at Headingley, the luckless Terry was retained for the Old Trafford Test, where he took the full force of a Winston Davis leather bullet flush on his forearm and suffered a fracture that put him out for the rest of the season.

Peter Sainsbury: Paul Terry is one of the most talented all-round sportsmen I have seen. He could be a county squash player, is outstanding at lawn tennis and is a superb striker of a golf ball. I'm just glad he chose cricket.

Terry's injury came only a month after Andy Lloyd had been struck on the head by a ball from Malcolm Marshall in the First Test which put him out for the rest of the season with blurred vision in his right eye.

Alan Oakman says of Lloyd:

He was a gift to us, and to be honest he should be playing for Worcestershire. They had him on their books but lost interest.

We first noticed Andy when we took our Under-25 side to Oswestry. We expected to do well, but this little ginger chap came out and scored a stack of runs against us. He wasn't particularly elegant, but he pushed and ran and looked as though he knew what he was doing. He reminded me a lot of Ken Suttle, who opened with me at Sussex. One of our side, Phil Oliver, said that the lad had played for Worcester Seconds and, as we don't go around poaching players, I didn't think any more of him.

About a fortnight went by, and then Phil rang me and said that Andy had called him up to say that Worcestershire had not invited him back. Andy was furious. He had scored a lot of runs for them, including a century. Then he went off to college for a time to further his education in case he failed at cricket. Eventually he came back to us and played in the Birmingham League where he built up a phenomenal average of 160. I keep telling our players that if they score runs in the Birmingham League they are bound to get publicity.

Andy is one of those chaps who speaks his mind. He can be quite volatile at times. It certainly doesn't pay to upset him. And he's a complete Jekyll and Hyde when it comes to being organised. Out on the field he is absolutely perfect, but once he gets to the dressing-room he's the worry of my life. All hell is let loose. He's always looking for a boot, or a sock, or he can't find his box. He's the most disorganised player I've ever met off the field. And he loves a joke, though usually at someone else's expense! He loves to take the Mickey out of people.

We are delighted with him. He's a fine player, and with another year's experience under his belt he should go right to the top.

Good fortune certainly smiled on Oakman when meeting up with Lloyd, and a similar slice of luck helped him towards the signing of Lloyd's opening partner David (K.D.) Smith.
Alan Oakman: We were drawn to play the winners of a Gillette Cup match between Northumberland and Lincoln, so our secretary Alan Smith, who was captain then, thought I should go up to Cumbria to watch the game. When it was all over I went to the bar, and from where I was sitting I could see a few lads playing cricket in the far corner of the ground.

Ken Smith, the former Leicestershire player, came to sit with me and I said, 'That lad with the bat looks a good player.'

'That's my son,' he said.

It turned out that David was nineteen and playing in the Northern League. So I invited him down for a trial, and from the very first day he showed that he was an outstanding player of fast bowling.

David is always technically correct. Always playing straight. Very quiet, and totally single-minded. A model professional. When it comes to fielding, he struggles a bit, and he knows it. In three-day games he's useful in the slips, but in the one-day matches he's not needed there, and it's difficult to hide him.

Later on, David's younger brother Paul joined us from the Lord's groundstaff, and he's another strong batsman, and with an aggressive attitude to life. Two years at Lord's under Don Wilson definitely helped to discipline him, but there is still a little work for us to do in that department.

Experience has shown that in cricket it can often pay to have more than one member of the same family on your staff. The Comptons, Chappells, Greigs and Crowes are all good examples. Sign one brother and look at the other, that's my motto.

Asif Din also came to us from Lord's, though I'm afraid he's struggled a bit against the seamers. In my day we used to say, 'See the two quickies off and then we can relax a little.' Against Yorkshire we used to say, 'See Fred off and we'll get among them.' Today it is seamer after seamer. There is no breather, and people like Asif don't get the chance to play their full range of shots.

Engulfed in turmoil almost for as long as the mind can remember, Yorkshire members finally pledged overwhelming support for Geoff Boycott in April 1984 and precipitated the departure of manager Ray Illingworth, the appointment of Brian Close as chairman of the cricket committee, and the ousting of Fred Trueman as an area representative.

Careful not to commit himself too precisely, Doug Padgett says of Boycott:

He is a very fine player. When you are talking about a batsman's technique you will go a long way to find a better one. He gets himself into such good positions. And he does so well on difficult wickets. That's where a batsman's class shows up. That's where his technique comes to the rescue.

Players who get runs on a difficult pitch are a Godsend. Being able to play on lifting, turning wickets is a gift. One of Boycott's best knocks was against Derbyshire on a difficult track in Sheffield. His technique got him through when everyone else failed.

Boycott's a thorough professional. In that respect he sets a good example. No one living could be more dedicated to the game. And he's always willing to help if a young lad wants advice; though he can be a bit blunt. He gives an honest opinion, and that's all anyone can expect.

The spotlight has been on him a great deal with all our troubles. We seem to have had one problem after another. I've hated it all, though I think a lot of the trouble has been exaggerated. We seem to attract publicity. People like to keep stirring the pot where we are concerned. (*That pot was boiling again in 1984 when Close resigned after clashes over Boycott.*)

As for the loss of Bill Athey to Gloucestershire in 1984, it transpires that this was not just a blow to Yorkshire, but a huge personal disappointment to Yorkshire coach Doug Padgett, who explains:
When I first saw Bill Athey he was only fourteen. I had just finished in county cricket and was playing for Marske as a professional in the North Yorkshire and Durham League. I remember we had a match against Saltburn and I saw this little lad coming out to bat. As the professional, I was expected to bowl a bit, but this boy impressed me so much I deliberately tried not to get him out. Then I brought him down to the Yorkshire nets and he went on to play for England. When he left us I was naturally very upset, because we had been together for so long and been such good friends.

Bill is a good example of the way we find our young players. Then, having brought them up to championship standard, we have to start all over again. It's a never-ending process. Only three players in our 1984 county side didn't come up through me – Geoff Boycott, David Bairstow and Richard Lumb. I have known the others since they were kids.

All through the years Sussex have matched the very best in the world of wicketkeeping. Billy Griffith, Jim Parks and then the imported Arnold Long, from Surrey, all maintained a standard no member wanted to see lowered. So when Parks went along with his son,

7

Bobby, a fine wicketkeeping prospect, it was taken for granted in many quarters that the lad was going to continue the family trend. But it was not to be. Bobby was turned down and he moved on to Hampshire, leaving Sussex to scramble around to find someone to meet their high standards.

Stewart Storey: The committee had a straight choice between Bobby and Tim Head. They stuck by Tim, and Bobby was allowed to leave. Arnold Long was still our first-team wicketkeeper but he was nearing the end of his career. When Arnold retired, we started negotiations with Paul Downton, who was being allowed to leave Kent. Downton, however, decided to join Middlesex which, in turn, persuaded us to look at the Middlesex wicketkeeper Ian Gould, who was young, and a ready-made cricketer.

Gould was my first signing and, as often happens in such cases, we took on a chap who was on the rebound and felt he had a point to prove. He was given a golden opportunity to do well, and was selected for England's 1983 tour of Australia, but he blew it. He was too lazy. He didn't get stuck in. And he has now lost all chance of commanding a regular place as England's number-one wicketkeeper.

At his best, Ian is sharp and agile, though he does tend to get overweight, which slows his reactions. His main problem is that he shows a professional attitude to the game, but not to his own performance.

Over the past thirty to forty years Kent, probably more than any other county, have produced one star wicketkeeper after another. There seems no end to their supply. After the amazing Les Ames came Godfrey Evans, then Alan Knott, Derek Ufton and Downton, and now two more outstanding prospects, Stephen Marsh and Stuart Waterton, are virtually sleeping in their pads waiting for the chance to press home their claims for a regular place in the county side.

Colin Page: Alan Knott looked an England certainty when he was just fourteen. He could have come on our staff as a batsman, bowler or a wicketkeeper. In fact, he had to bowl for a few years because we had Godfrey Evans and Derek Ufton doing so well behind the stumps.

Paul Downton also came to us as a schoolboy. His father was a fine wicketkeeper and Paul has more than emulated him. What's more, Paul is a much better batsman than he has shown so far. I was very disappointed when he left us for Middlesex, but with Alan Knott playing so well, I understood how he felt about wanting a regular first-team place.

For no obvious reason Gloucestershire, like Kent, are frequently embarrassed by the number of talented wicketkeepers who continue to queue up for recognition. In present times Jack Russell, Andy Brassington and Andy Stovold are all capable of holding a regular county place.

Graham Wiltshire: Jack Russell came to us as a nipper. He was a natural. He had good hands, moved well, and was extremely fast. Brassington came from Bristol schools. We had a batsman on the staff who played against Andy, and he came back full of praise.

'Well, what was he like?' I asked.

'He talks too much,' came the reply.

'How were you out?'

'Stumped down the leg side off the quickie.'

I had heard enough. I invited Brassington over for a trial and I took him to the nets and deliberately bowled two balls down the leg side. He not only caught them brilliantly, but took the bails off as well. I knew then that he was a bit special.

I always say that a good wicketkeeper is the fellow who can take the ball consistently well when an off-spinner is bowling to a right-hander.

Surrey, too, have lately been short of a good wicketkeeper, with Arthur McIntyre, Arnold Long and the current incumbent, Jack Richards, all exceptionally capable performers.

David Gibson: Jack Richards plays a large part in controlling matches for us. Only he can see all the angles the batsmen play through. He reads the game extremely well and is a first-class communicator. He is a big help to our bowlers because he sees the line of the ball better than they do themselves. When a bowler shouts for an lbw decision, he is seldom, if ever, in the best position to judge. Bowlers run off the wicket when they release the ball, so only the umpire and wicket-keeper are left in a direct line and can tell whether an appeal is justified.

Just to mention the word wicketkeeper brings Nottinghamshire manager Ken Taylor swiftly to the talented Bruce French.

A county debut at the young age of 16 years 287 days launched French on a career which accelerated rapidly in 1984 when the selectors chose him as Paul Downton's deputy on the winter tour of India.

Ken Taylor: Bruce is a beautiful wicketkeeper, though I must say he's been a bit tricky at times. He's needed the occasional kick up the rear-end.

He's a scream really. He first made me laugh when he was chosen as Nottinghamshire's Young Wicketkeeper of the Year. The prize was a fortnight in Cyprus, and the first thing we had to do was kit him out with a full range of clothes. Then he came along and sheepishly asked if he could take someone with him.

I said, 'Of course. What's all the fuss?'

He said, 'It's a girl. And I've got to get her off school!'

She was about fifteen and I finished up calling on the headmaster to get her released. Bruce has married her now and they have two children.

Then there was another occasion when we played Northampton in a Benson and Hedges match. He did so well that Godfrey Evans poked his head around the dressing-room door and said to Bruce, 'Well done. You kept beautifully. A very good show. Go on like that and you'll play for England.'

Then, after Godfrey had left, Bruce turned to the lads and said, 'Who the hell was that geezer?'

His only fault is that he doesn't shout enough at our bowlers and fielders, though he is getting better. He should tick them off more. I suppose he's found it difficult with so many older players in the side. Bob Taylor has been a big help. Bruce always goes to him when a problem comes up.

Next-door neighbours Derbyshire also provided extra power when Mike Hendrick decided to move thirty miles down the road to Trent Bridge.

Ken Taylor: I heard along the grapevine that Mike wanted to come to us, so I offered him a contract. Somerset were also in the market for him, but we were handy. It meant he didn't have to move house.

One thing I must emphasise is that I don't cheat. I don't go up to players and dangle carrots. But there's no point in people kidding themselves at Lord's, because players do tell other players if they fancy a move. So if a player comes to me and says he knows of someone who wants to leave another county because he's not happy, I always insist that it is done in the right way. The player concerned must go to his club first. At no time do I say, 'Rubbish, I'm not interested.' That would be nonsense. I know full well that another county would jump in once my back was turned.

Being in the right place at the right time also enabled Taylor to be first in line for Chris Broad, the tall, powerful opening batsman who was at loggerheads with Gloucestershire.
Ken Taylor: It was pennies from heaven. I was terribly worried about not having an opener for Tim Robinson. Basharat Hassan was going in first, but it was not satisfactory for him or for us. We were playing Gloucestershire at Bristol and their captain David Graveney came up and said that Chris Broad was going and that if I wanted to approach him no one would object. I jumped at the chance. Chris had looked very promising. He was also a left-hander, which was a bonus. We were short of left-handers. I knew that if he got used to our wickets, which bounce a lot more than they do at Bristol, he could do a good job for us.

Broad, of course, fulfilled every optimistic prediction and even catapulted himself into the England team in just three months after completing the move to Trent Bridge.
Again with the help of his friends, Ken Taylor's recruiting skills were responsible for both Eddie Hemmings and Mike Bore settling for a new niche at Nottingham. Of the Hemmings transfer, he admits:
Having heard that Eddie was going to be available, I telephoned the Warwickshire chairman, whom I knew quite well as we had played together before the war. At first he said that Eddie had been offered a further year's contract, but a week later he telephoned me to say that Eddie had turned it down. I was then given permission to approach him, which meant I had a week's start on everyone else.

We badly needed an off-spinner and I fancied Eddie a lot.

In particular I remembered the day he took all ten wickets against us in a second-team match.

He is a good player, though he does have his peculiarities. And there are times when he might look portly and overweight, but this has nothing to do with lack of training. Eddie suffers from asthma, and the tablets he takes tend to blow up his stomach.

Signing Mike Bore was another stroke of good fortune. I have an excellent relationship with the Yorkshire committee who gave me the wink that he wanted a new county, and I didn't waste a minute before moving in.

Of course, having an established first team can often be frustrating for a county coach who is always eager to find the best opportunities for young players coming up under his care. Doug Padgett is certainly one person who isn't sorry to see the occasional door open at Yorkshire to let his new lads in. He explains:

I have to keep people happy when they can't move up. Take the wicketkeeping department, for instance. There is no way a lad can come in with David Bairstow there. He's had the spot for the past twelve years, and rightly so. We had a lad called Steven Rhodes, a very competent 'keeper, and a good batsman. A young lad itching to get on. But what could we do with him? How long could we ask him to wait? In the end he moved on to Worcester. Bairstow is only thirty-three. He could be here for many more years. So if Rhodes had stayed he could have had a long wait on his hands. That can be terribly daunting for someone who dearly wants to play for his county, and is good enough.

We can usually find a place for an extra batsman. It's the specialists who suffer. A wicketkeeper or a left-arm spinner. If you have a crackerjack in those positions, then the second in line is struggling a bit. In time he will probably move on.

This is frustrating for me. Having found a lad, I want to keep him. Sometimes I run out of luck. Just when an established player decides to retire, I find that I have no one standing by to take his place. Two years earlier I might have had the ideal chap, but he's now doing his stuff with someone else.

We are well stocked with good players at the moment. It's

great to be here. Martyn Moxon and Kevin Sharp are two fine batsmen who must have a big future ahead of them.

Moxon was fifteen when I first saw him. Then I followed his progress through the schools and brought him along in the second team where he played for five years, with the occasional outing in the county side. When he played in the first team, he did very well. Then for the 1984 season, we decided he should open with Geoff Boycott in all championship matches. Moxon is a first-class professional. He is not only a good player, but has a marvellous temperament. And he applies himself well.

A recurrent rib injury cost Moxon two Test chances against the West Indians, but he finally answered the call when selected for the 1984–85 winter tour of India and Australia.

Over at Leicester, Ken Higgs is particularly pleased at the co-operation he receives from his players, especially the younger ones.

All my lads give me 110 per cent, and young James Whittaker has delighted me as much as anyone. Having scored runs galore at school, he came into our second team in 1983, which was a big step up for him. Worse still, we were playing Worcestershire, and their quickie Hartley Alleyne was bowling down the hill. James opened the innings, and Alleyne's very first ball uprooted his middle stump. The lad never moved. He just froze to the spot.

When he came back I put my arm around his shoulder and said, 'James, you must forget that altogether. It has gone. There is nothing you can do about it.'

So the second innings came round and I said to him, 'Right, James, the same bowler is out there, but he's only human like you. Open your legs. Reach.'

And Alleyne bounced him with his very first ball. It nearly knocked his head off. He turned white. But from then on, the lad never looked back. He realised he was playing with men. His schooldays were over. And he went on to score fifty.

That innings did him a power of good. He made up his mind that no one was going to get him out. He's a strong boy who used to play all his shots through mid-wicket. Now he knows where the off side is. He's learning all the time. He turned from a boy into a man in less than two days. That, to me, is the best baptism possible for any young player. If he couldn't cope with that type of pressure there is no way he would make a living from this game.

During 1983 Andy Miller and Colin Metson were two fine players on the brink of a regular place in the Middlesex side, and Don Bennett said of them:

Miller came up through our Colts and went to Oxford. He's a good opener with an excellent temperament. Metson is a fine young wicketkeeper who also came up through our Colts. He is learning a lot from Paul Downton, who sets a marvellous example to all our young players. Paul works hard at his skills. Batting is getting his fullest concentration at present. He was strokeless when he came here, but he's starting to develop a few shots now.

Kent had Paul first, but Alan Knott was there so his chances were limited. Then we heard that one of them was being released. We though it must be Knott, as he was the older man, but when we discovered it was Paul, Mike Brearley and I went out to watch him. Of course, we were impressed, and a week or so later we invited him up to an interview. He actually came here with an agent, but he presented himself so well he didn't need anyone at his side to give advice. Sussex also wanted him, so we knew we had a fight on our hands. To be candid, we didn't expect him to come. Then a few weeks later he rang up and said he wanted to join us.

Ian Gould was still keeping wicket in our first team and, though he began the 1980 season well, he gradually went off the boil and that's when Paul first came into the reckoning. I also suggested that he should go in first, and he responded well and strung a few good innings together.

As wicketkeepers go, there is little between them. Gould is a good judge of players, and so is Downton. I thought the world of Gould and I picked his brains. But Paul is a terrific asset.

Meanwhile at Worcester, Basil d'Oliveira admits to being excited by the phalanx of young talent he now has maturing under his strict leadership, especially with players like Richard Illingworth, Martin Weston and his own son, Damian. Speaking about Illingworth, d'Oliveira says:

He is a very promising left-arm spinner, and every side should have one. I would never go into a match without one. But Richard has been rushed. After a season in Australia he was pushed straight into our first team when Norman Gifford left. In just two to three years of county cricket he has done as much as some bowlers do in ten.

Playing on Australian wickets helped him a lot because he needed a different style and a different approach. But when he came back he tended to stop in his delivery. He got to the wicket very slowly, and the ball drifted through the air at the same gentle pace. He needed to put more energy and effort into his bowling, and he is doing that well now.

Being rushed into the side could affect his confidence. He may fail to produce the goods and some people may start calling for his head. The spotlight will be on him. While he is learning, he is bound to take some hammer. That's when people must stick by him. They must be patient. I am sure they will be in three-day games, but it's the one-day matches that worry me. That's when everyone wants instant success.

It's going to be tough for him because he's not ready for the first team yet. I don't see him becoming anything like a top-class player for a further two to three years. But I shall back him. And I know we have others here who understand enough about the game who will also back him.

Spin bowling is a hard business. Sometimes it can take up to six or seven years for a spinner to learn his trade.

In my time there was no one-day cricket. Players had the chance to gain experience. They could spend up to four years in the second team, learning the job. But now if a player can whack the ball over the top, or bowl three balls an over in the blockhole, he's in the first team overnight and he doesn't do his apprenticeship. So unless a player can adjust to all the different games he will go to pieces.

Illingworth had a dream start. He bowled against Viv Richards and Ian Botham and got them both out. It was a big occasion for him, but he adapted well. He bowled flatter and tighter against them. He used his brains.

My son Damian has also pleased me a lot. He spent two years on the Lord's groundstaff under Don Wilson, and a year in Australia. So he came through on his own. I saw it as an opportunity for him to learn the game away from his dad. It also helped him develop his character and personality.

When Damian first mentioned that he would like to play county cricket I said, 'Fine. No problem. But wouldn't it be wiser if you went away from Worcester to do it?'

He said, 'No. I'd rather stay here.'

So I told him, 'Look, you know that I'm going to be here for the rest of my life, so wouldn't it be better if someone else gave you a trial?' And he again said, 'No. I want to play for Worcester.' He had made up his mind. So I said, 'Fine. Great.'

But we made one stipulation. We agreed that when we left the ground in the evening there would be no inquests. Come half-past six, all talk of cricket would stop. What had to be said would be said at the ground. We wouldn't take our jobs home with us.

When he scored a hundred against Middlesex, I wasn't there. So I rang him up and congratulated him. I simply said, 'Well done.' Then, when I arrived home that night, I said, 'Did you enjoy it?' He said 'Yes. It was just that I should have gone on longer.' And that was it. There was no lengthy discussion. We talk, obviously. We don't cut ourselves off altogether. But there are no arguments. If something needs to be sorted out, we do that at the ground between ten o'clock and six-thirty.

I am proud of him. He has come through on his own. He has a good temperament. Nothing worries him. He is very much like me in that respect. In some ways he is better than me, though he can be a bit too casual at times.

Sons of famous fathers often have an impossible task. Ron Headley got pig sick of being known as 'the son of George'. Richard Hutton suffered badly as the son of Sir Len. And Bradman's son was so incensed he even changed his name.

Damian is a very co-ordinated person. I noticed this when he was about ten, though I knew he had to be a lot better than me to survive in his own right. He had to overcome my name. I don't know how he's coped with that, because I've never really asked him, but there's little doubt that he has.

Peter Robinson was well established as Somerset's chief coach when a young man called Ian Terrence Botham first played for the county in 1973. Robinson remembers it well:

At first, Ian used to hop on a train and come down from London to play in our second team. He was on the Lord's groundstaff, and Len Muncer had a lot of influence on him up there. To be honest, we thought more of Ian's batting then. He played one John Player League game for us in 1973 and came on the staff the following year.

When he started, I took him around with me to help him settle in. Even then he was always very confident, very sure of himself. I think that's one of his great assets. He presents himself as being larger than life. I noticed it in the middle from the start. Most players who bowl four long-hops usually worry about where the next two are going to pitch, but not Ian. He is still thinking of taking two wickets. In that position I would be happy for the batsman to push the ball back. But Ian is not that type of cricketer. He wants something to happen all the time. And he's prepared to make it happen.

His big breakthrough came against Andy Roberts at Taunton. We were playing Hampshire in a Benson and Hedges match and Roberts hit Ian under the jaw. It was a sickening blow, but he wasn't bothered. He just stood there and attacked. He scored about forty and saw us through in a nail-biting finish. That was the first time I saw his true character. He was willing to fight and have a go, and that's been the feature of his cricket ever since.

People say that Ian should take more care. Play more gracefully. Stroke the ball around. That's nonsense. I try to tell them that if we restrain and restrict him, we will take away his greatest natural aptitude. If we are 60 for 6, he will want to go out and take the game apart. He will want to swing his bat. That's the way he plays. No one expects him to be technically perfect, because he's not.

When Ian took over as England captain he had a rough time. He came back to our nets and I noticed that his 'pick-up' had strayed. Having played in ten Test matches against the West Indians and faced so much short bowling, he was tending to pick up towards gully and play across the line. So we talked about it and I left it at that. Then we went off to play

Sussex. Imran and Garth Le Roux were playing and they got us in dead trouble. We were being shot out when Ian went in and pulled and hooked and scored seventy magnificent runs.

Then, with just ten minutes left, he was caught trying to hook. So I went to the dressing-room and I said, 'Well, Ian, fancy getting out at that time.'

And he smiled at me and said, 'But I picked up straighter, didn't I ?'

Oh, I thought, he had noticed.

I know Ian gives the impression that he doesn't think about his cricket, but he does. He knows the game.

We made him captain in 1984, and we knew he would be entirely different from anyone we had appointed before. But the players respected him and responded to him, and he thrived on the responsibility. He really wanted to prove he could captain a side.

Let's face it, he captained England at the worst possible time. No matter who would have been in charge then, he would have struggled to get results. It was cannons versus pea-shooters. Ian was on a hiding to nothing.

We had one or two players who needed to be jostled a bit. Ian was just the man to sort them out. He would say, 'Right, you've been promising for two to three years, so here's the ball, and here's the bat, now let's see what you can do.'

A great deal has been said about Ian's fitness over the years. Well, the truth is he's had a lot of trouble with his back and this has affected his bowling. He became technically wrong, and even more open in his action. His body dropped away as he bowled, and he lost his knack of making the ball swing.

Ian has played a lot of cricket when he was badly unfit. Nothing could have been easier for him than to come back from a strenuous Test match and say, 'Look lads, I'm not fit. Leave me out.' But he's never done that. He's always gone out there and done his best for the club. With broken toes, chipped fingers, pulled muscles – heaven knows what. Such dedication, of course, can work against a player sometimes. If he carries on when he's not fit, his standards will probably drop. That's what happened to Ian. And people started to say he was finished.

Ian played on when he should have been resting. He went

through the motions of bowling. Worse still, he aggravated his injuries.

Of course, we all know he's worked a lot. England have treated him as lunch and tea. They've bowled him into the ground. There were times when they bowled him for thirty overs in a day. He was always on the field. Always in the action. The machine was never switched off. He was bound to burn himself out.

Ian took a lot of stick for playing football before going on that disastrous England tour of New Zealand and Pakistan, but that's Ian. He wants to be up on the stage. Obviously we would like to see him give up football, but he's not on contract to us in winter. He's a free agent. He can do what he likes. And he usually does.

As the prognosticators scratch their heads and hesitatingly predict who will emerge from the mass to replace the tiring Ian Botham as England's next complete all-rounder, Brian Reynolds is convinced it could be David Capel, born and reared in Northamptonshire, and maturing with every match:

This lad has enormous ability. The trouble is, he's a bit headstrong at the moment, so I have to keep telling him to set his sights on being an England all-rounder. To have a target. If he puts his mind to it, I am sure he will go right to the top.

We also have Robert Bailey, who has tremendous potential. As a bowler, his only technical fault is that he lands on the so-called wrong foot. I thought of correcting him, but he's bowled that way for so long now that I'm afraid I might confuse him. I also keep thinking of Mike Procter. After all, he bowled off the 'wrong' foot and became a superstar.

As a batsman Robert still tends to hit the ball in the air, yet when he took 190 off Essex Seconds, the only time he skied one was when he was caught at mid-on. He has proved that he can keep the ball on the ground provided he puts his mind to it.

Of course, behind the stars in every county side are the dependable players – the people who work hard, contribute enormously yet rarely, if ever, hit the headlines. They are the backbone of a team. Brian Reynolds spoke about the Northamptonshire players who fall into this category:

19

The big Jims, Griffiths and Yardley, are two of ours. Griffiths is a magnificent, whole-hearted bowler. He took more wickets in our second team than anyone before him. Yardley is the best catcher I have ever seen. And a very aggressive batsman who can turn a game in two overs. He's often our unsung hero in one-day matches. These are the type of bread-and-butter players no county can do without. The dedicated sort who keep us alive.

Ex-policeman Geoff Humpage switched from catching criminals on the beat to grabbing thin edges as Warwickshire's fine wicketkeeper, though he had plenty to learn at first, as Alan Oakman explains:

His biggest problem early on was coping with Eddie Hemmings's spin on a turning pitch. But we persevered with him. We gave him a second chance and he went from strength to strength, though his batting was always good enough for him to press for a regular place.

Before he joined us Geoff was pursuing a career in the Birmingham Police force. Their cricket team used to come to our nets, and when I saw him batting I thought he was too good not to be in first-class cricket. I told our committee that he was wasting his time as a policeman and we invited him to play in our second team. His inspector wasn't too pleased about that and told him that he had to choose between being a copper and a cricketer. Since then his success as an international player has proved that he chose wisely.

In my time a wicketkeeper was always selected for his wicketkeeping alone, but now, when I am told there is a wicketkeeper worth watching, the first thing I say is 'Can he bat?'

When it comes to engaging good players from outside his county there is no mistaking Don Bennett's remarkable luck. For it was only through friends and good fortune that Middlesex acquired such fine players as Phil Edmonds, John Emburey, Norman Cowans and Wilf Slack, to name just four.

Edmonds had signed for Kent; Emburey was playing with Surrey; Slack was an unknown batsman in High Wycombe; and Cowans was a schoolboy who literally came in from the cold.

*Don Bennett:*It was Majid Khan, the Pakistani batsman, who put me on to Phil Edmonds. Middlesex were hunting high and low for a good spinner at the time. I happened to meet Majid at Lord's, and he said that he had played with a chap called Edmonds at Cambridge who looked very promising. I took his word for that, but when I started asking questions I discovered that Edmonds was actually on Kent's books and had played in their second team. Kent, of course, had Derek Underwood, so they agreed to release Philip once they knew we were interested, though we had to put up a fight because Warwickshire also fancied him.

Philip actually started out as a quick bowler, and changed to slow at Cambridge. Even now he can generate a lot of pace, especially if someone upsets him. He surprised the New Zealanders in 1982 with a few that flew around their ears before Richard Hadlee took revenge with some well-chosen blows.

Philip has been something of an enigma in Test cricket. He's found it hard to make an impact at that level. Yet when the chips are down with us he usually produces the goods, which makes it more of a mystery why he can't come up trumps for England.

Injuries have also troubled him badly, particularly his back. He used to hang himself upside down on a traction machine to treat a disc problem, and a wag was once heard to suggest that he should try hanging from his neck.

The Press have made a lot of Philip upsetting colleagues with his impish comments in the England and Middlesex dressing rooms, but I have absolute respect for him. We've always got on well. Potentially he is the best left-arm spinner I have seen.

Moving on to John Emburey's fortuitous transfer, Bennett recalls that it was Arthur McIntyre, Surrey's outstanding wicketkeeper of the fifties, whom Middlesex had to thank for bringing this brilliant off-spinner to their notice:
Emburey had played for Surrey Schools and had set his heart on playing senior cricket for his county. But Surrey had Pat Pocock, and McIntyre thought John was too good to waste in the shadows. So he rang me up and said, 'Don, we've got a

good off-spinner down here, but we can't take him on. Would you like to see him?'

At Middlesex of course we had Titmus, but he was older than Pocock, so I thought it would be sensible to look at his lad.

A week later Emburey came to our nets, and after he had bowled five or six balls, I said to him, 'That's all right, lad. That will do. I've seen enough.'

His face went white.

'Oh, God,' he said. 'It was hardly worth coming.'

And I smiled at him. 'Don't be daft,' I said. 'It's not a bit like that. I've seen enough to take you on.'

Though I knew his heart was still set on playing for Surrey, I was delighted to sign him.

John has an excellent cricket brain. He's probably the best off-spinner in the world. And his batting has also improved.

I remember when he first came to us he batted at number eleven. He was terrible. I played in one second-team match with him against Sussex, and we had to bat out time to save the game. Sussex had a medium-pacer called Denman, and I remember John coming down the wicket to me and saying, 'In no way am I going to face that chap. He's too quick.'

Now he can face any bowler, Daniel and Cowans included. He has made himself into a very useful number six, though some people are only just beginning to accept it. He has done it all himself, through working hard.

The signing of Wilf Slack bordered on a fairy story. It happened after wicketkeeper Ian Gould had lost form and asked Bennett if he could turn out for Slough Thursdays to sharpen himself up.

Don Bennett: It was one of my rare quiet days so I decided to go along and watch. There was just one other spectator on the ground, and it happened to be Alan Huntley, who had played with me at High Wycombe before I went back to Middlesex as coach.

While we sat and watched, Alan told me of this 'tremendous' young coloured boy called Slack at High Wycombe who could become a county player if given the chance. Alan thought I should run my eye over him, and because it was Alan talking I knew the lad must be good. Alan wasn't the type who went around over-praising people, and I knew he was a fine judge.

A week later our Under-25 side was due to play Kent at Blackheath and I found I was a batsman short. So I telephoned Alan and arranged for Slack to meet me at Marylebone Railway station.

Kent batted first and we got them out for 180. I went straight into the dressing-room and said, 'Wilfred, I want you to go in first.'

He looked at me and froze. He couldn't believe his ears. Then I watched him glance around the room at the other players. At chaps like Gatting, Butcher, Gomes, Gould and Emburey.

Then he turned to me and said, 'I can't go in first.'

'Right,' I said. 'If you don't go in first, you will go in at number nine.' So he put his pads on and went in.

Kent fielded a strong side and Kevin Jarvis opened their bowling. His first ball to Slack was a half-volley and he cracked it for four. He never looked in danger. He was still there when we reached the last eight overs. Gatting went to the wicket and I told him, 'Don't do anything potty. Tell Slack to play a few shots, but not to throw his wicket away.'

Slack finished with 80 not out, and we won by eight wickets. He couldn't have dreamt of a better start.

Slack was working for an electronics firm at the time and was only free to play in our one-day midweek matches. Despite this, he averaged something like seventy, so I took him on.

At that stage I had never seen him play spin, and I soon learned that he couldn't play it at all. But as time went on, both Edmonds and Emburey helped him in the nets and he has improved a lot now. He is also a useful medium-pacer to have in the side, particularly in the one-day games.

England's frantic search for a reliable pace bowler centred on Derbyshire for a short time in 1983 when Paul Newman looked set to press for an international place. But just when Newman was coming to his peak, a string of injuries robbed him of a golden opportunity to emphasise his claim. Phil Russell recalls Newman's appalling luck:

Richard Hadlee started it all when he struck Paul on the foot and broke a bone, though Paul played on for a fortnight without telling anyone. He was desperate to stay in the team, although it was obvious something was wrong because he was down to three-quarter pace. He took a long time to recover, and when he eventually came back he took six wickets for seven runs, in an Under-25 match against Notts.

At last he's right, I thought. But just as we were pencilling him in for a return to the first team, he burst a blood vessel and his arm swelled up like a balloon. More rest was needed, and when he came back again only five weeks of the season were left, and he bowled just 88 overs and took seven wickets.

County cricket is not as relaxed as it used to be, and I'm sure many injuries are being caused by tension. If a side has to win, the bowler's action is not the same. He is tense. It is the same tension that you see in snooker, or in the putt at golf, or in the tennis shot when a player is going for a winner. Players must learn to overcome this feeling. But it's not easy. In fact, it is part of my job to help them remove any element of fear – to stop them from thinking, 'If I don't take five wickets today, I'm out of the team.'

For blatant cheek and determination few players can match the bold John Morris, who deserves all the runs that are now coming his way as a maturing Derbyshire batsman.

Absolutely confident in his own ability, Morris refused to be put off when seeking a trial with Derbyshire. He was determined to show them what he could do, as Phil Russell recalls:

John wrote in for a trial, and I said we couldn't see him that week because we were at Old Trafford.

'All right,' he said, 'I'll come up there for a net!'

With push like that, how could I turn him down? So he came along and I saw him bat on a bad wicket. And he was so good I picked him for our next second-team game.

Morris, who is twenty, made his debut in 1982 and by 1984 was a regular member of the county side.

With the indestructible Bob Taylor seemingly going on for ever and ever, finding a deputy wicketkeeper with comparable skills has proved a prodigious problem, though Bernard Maher is now ready and capable of answering the call.

Phil Russell: We've tried eight wicketkeepers, and Maher is the best. We've offered him a longer contract and we hope he'll take over now that Bob has retired. He has sharp reactions, strong fingers and is very agile. And he has a degree in accountancy, so he's got brains, as well. With Bob away on Test duty so much, Bernard has gained a fair bit of experience. And he's no fool with the bat. We asked him to open against Somerset and he scored 52.

This emphasis on team-building is crucial as Derbyshire seek to control their escalating wage bill. In 1976 it was just £16,800; in 1981 – £47,000; and in 1984 it had rocketed to £110,000, with a playing staff of eighteen. Optimism runs high about young men like Dallas Moir, Iain Anderson and Roger Finney.

Phil Russell: Geoff Miller discovered Dallas playing for Scotland. He liked his slow left-armers and thought he would replace David Steele, which he did. Dallas is a giant of a man. He stands 6ft 8in., about the same height as Joel Garner, and can be very difficult to face.

In a roundabout way, Eddie Barlow must take the credit for finding Iain Anderson. Financial problems had forced us to disband our second team for three years, but Eddie begged us to start it up again. To get it off the ground, I signed up five youngsters, and Anderson was the one who came through. He's only twenty-four, and he scored 1,200 runs in 1983.

Roger Finney came to us straight from the Lord's groundstaff. He bowls left-arm medium-pace and swings it a lot. He can also bat. In fact all our players bat and bowl. That's what makes them such fine cricketers. I remember Leicestershire winning the championship with eleven players who could bat and bowl. They had a staff of thirteen, and at one stage they had three left-arm spinners, two off-spinners and five seamers.

To balance youth with experience, John Hampshire was brought in from Yorkshire to bolster the batting.

Phil Russell: We slipped John into the number four spot, which gave us an all-Test first five with Wright, Wood, Kirsten and Miller. The trouble was, we couldn't bowl sides out. In one season Wright and Kirsten scored fifteen centuries between them, but we won only three matches. Then we changed our policy and tried to have a better bowling side, to have a better balance. And it worked.

Ironically, while Northamptonshire have combed the world for outstanding cricketers, little Richard Williams, at 5ft. 6in. one of the shortest players in the game, has made so much progress that the England selectors short-listed him for their 1982 tour of Australia and chose him for the MCC side that opened the 1984 season against champions Essex. Welshman Williams, who played for Northants Seconds when only fourteen, has matured under the watchful, yet critical eye of Brian Reynolds, who admits that their relationship has not always been harmonious:

For a long time it was a love-hate relationship. Richard kept annoying me because he didn't have the discipline to get to the top. He used to spin the ball a lot, but he couldn't pitch it. So I kept taking him to the nets and telling him, 'For heaven's sake, you must eliminate the bad ball.'

I spent hours and hours with him. He was my main bowler in the second team. I admired him so much that I would take a fast bowler off as quickly as I could to get Richard on. After a time he learnt to bowl the drifter. The ball that runs away from the batsman. No spin bowler ever got to the top without it. Laker, Titmus, Tattersall, Savage . . . they all bowled the drifter.

Richard would have reached the top a lot earlier if he hadn't rammed his head into the back of a lorry while riding a motor-bike. That accident definitely held up his progress as a cricketer. Many times he has had to go off the field because of his terrible headaches, but he is fully recovered now, and there must be a fine future ahead for him.

Reynolds is also quick to praise Northamptonshire's shrewd Northern scout who continues to discover outstanding talent in the rich cricketing hotbeds of Yorkshire, Lancashire, and Durham, and then confidently send them South.

Geoff Cook, George Sharp, Neil Mallender, Peter Willey and now his latest discovery, Alan Walker, all slipped through the Northern net. Reynolds has nothing but praise for skipper Cook:

That man can't live without a bat in his hand. In his early

days, when he was not a regular in the first team, he was always pestering me for a game in the Seconds. I liked that. Geoff is totally dedicated and is always ready to help young players.

Unknown to many outside the committee, Cook went to the club as a slow left-armer. It was only later that he developed into a reliable opening batsman and was rewarded with a tour of Australia in 1982.

Like Cook, wicketkeeper Sharp is another capable left-arm spinner whose extra skills have been used on many occasions to baffle batsmen who didn't treat him with respect.

Brian Reynolds: From what I saw in the nets, Sharp looked a good bowler. Better than Cook. So I decided I would bring him into the attack whenever pitch conditions suited him.

The first time was against Glamorgan Seconds at Cardiff. We had set them about two hundred to win and then the wicket started to turn. Sharp was behind the stumps and Cook out in the covers. So I said to Sharp, 'Pull your pads off. Let Geoff take over. I want you to bowl.' And he finished with seven wickets, and we won with half a day to spare. Sharp's a bit of a secret weapon. I suppose it's a bit like having twelve players in the side.

When Mallender came here for a trial he was extremely aggressive. He had all the qualities a coach wants in a good quick bowler. And his attitude was right.

After a good start he hit some snags with his run-up, and that affected his form right through the 1983 season, when we thought he might be pushing for a place in the England team. We talked hard about what he was doing, and then realised that he wasn't bowling off the same foot every time. His rhythm was wrong. He had started to hesitate as he reached the stumps and lost confidence. When I pointed this out, he couldn't believe it. He couldn't remember doing it before. Having worked hard to rectify that fault, he is now looking good again. He also wants to bat, and has proved that he can get runs.

Alan Walker is the most recent speed bowler to join our ranks. As an ex-miner he is strong and powerful. If I had seen him earlier, I would have altered his action slightly, but it's too late now. He's in the groove, though I must get him to bowl closer to the stumps.

With England's anxious supporters wondering whether the reservoir is running dry of promising young players, Peter Robinson gives an emphatic 'No' as far as Somerset are concerned. Gary Palmer, Julian Wyatt, Mark Davis, Nigel Felton and Trevor Gard are all showing above-average potential.

Palmer, eighteen-year-old son of Ken Palmer, the former Somerset all-rounder and current Test-match umpire, is rated by many as the county's next Ian Botham.

Peter Robinson: Gary is showing a lot of promise. What he lacks is concentration. He gets in, looks good, and then ruins it all by playing a rash shot. He does silly things, which you expect from a lad of his age. When he puts his mind to it he is a useful all-rounder. He practises hard. And his father has helped him a lot, though they tend to squabble a bit too much.

Of Julian Wyatt, a flourishing opening batsman, Robinson recalls:

He did so well for our Under-19 side and in the Minor Counties that we took him on the staff in 1983. Julian kept ringing me up and asking 'What's happening? Can I come?'

Money was short at the time, so I had to push hard to get him a contract. He had impressed me a lot and I was worried another county might come in and pinch him from under our noses.

He came into the championship side for the last six games of that season and faced some of the fastest bowling in the world. He took on Malcolm Marshall twice, Winston Davis and Bob Willis. He hit forty off Marshall and the other Hampshire lads, and sixty off Davis and Glamorgan. He scored 338 runs for an average of 42.25 in five innings, with a top score of 82 not out.

Nothing bothers him. He has a marvellous temperament and he times the ball beautifully.

What pleases me is that after fighting for someone like that he has gone out and justified it. Hopefully we have backed a winner. I may still be wrong, but for the moment I can feel chuffed. It's like panning for gold, because so many lads come here for trials but very few impress.

Young Mark Davis came to light when Somerset advertised in a Taunton newspaper, saying 'Fast bowler wanted. Anyone and everyone welcome.' The response was so big that Robinson had to set aside a whole day to scrutinise the aspiring pacemen. It was Davis, a left-armer, who impressed him most:

Mark came into our first team and started in the best way possible, sending back a certain Mr Boycott for nought. What worries me about him is that he bowls well in his first spell, but doesn't come out for the second half. A lot of niggling injuries have also held him up, and I've told him he must work hard to maintain his fitness.

Somerset's patience was stretched to the limit before they finally signed the prospering Nigel Felton, and a grateful Robinson now says:

Like the sheriff in those old movies, I was determined to get my man. The trouble was, Nigel was on Kent's books, so I had to telephone Colin Page who told me nicely, 'Just keep your hands off!'

As often happens, word shot along the grapevine and Nigel wrote to me asking for a trial. At that point I telephoned Brian Luckhurst, the Kent manager, who thought Nigel had a lot of ability, and said he wouldn't stand in his way if we wanted to sign him. Nigel more than justified all that was said of him when he scored a superb 170 for us. And against Kent, too.

What we have never done is poach from other clubs and that is something of which we are proud.

With long-serving wicketkeeper Derek Taylor having put away his gloves, Somerset are ecstatic about the excellent form and promise of Trevor Gard.

Peter Robinson: Trevor's greatest virtue is patience. He has waited and waited for his chance. Dead man's shoes, almost. Trevor's big moment came at Lord's in 1983 when we beat Kent in the NatWest Final. His two stumpings were top quality. I have never doubted his wicketkeeping ability, but I was waiting to see how he reacted to the big occasion. He excelled. He proved he had the temperament for the major one-day games. That was the main thing, especially as we have something of a reputation to protect in this type of competition.

We all know that one swallow doesn't make a summer, but Trevor has already shown that he can become a tremendous asset for us. He once lived in the same area as Ian Botham, and they are good friends, which must be a big help. Ian and the lads encourage him. They all want him to do well. I know that if I had gone through the staff and asked who they wanted to have a good 1983, they would have said Trevor. They all willed it.

Of course, he follows a fine wicketkeeper in Derek, whose only mistake was being around at the same time as Bob Taylor and Alan Knott. I always rated Derek as England's number three. He came to us from Surrey and took over from Charlie Carter, whose father must have been friendly with the club president. Charlie struggled and we were in dire straits.

Derek was magnificent. And he made himself useful with the bat, even opening for a season or two until it became too much work, padding up all the time.

Colin Dredge and Nigel Popplewell are just two of many Somerset bowlers who have benefited from Taylor's constant help and advice:

Colin is a worker. A real willing horse. To be honest, his action has always been a bit awkward and he's never really looked the part, though he continues to produce some excellent get-out balls.

Colin didn't play much second-team cricket. He came in late. We found him bowling for Frome when we went into the Somerset leagues to see what was available. He has trained himself to be a good support bowler. And he's worked hard to keep his head up and his shoulder straight. He's a bread-and-butter bowler. And he's never let us down in the pressure of one-day games, despite having to come on at the end, at difficult times.

It was opener Peter Roebuck who brought Popplewell to Somerset's notice. They had played together at Cambridge and Roebuck recommended him just in time as two other counties were moving in.

Peter Robinson: Nigel has been a big-game player. He thrives in the one-day fixtures. If he could only produce the same performances in three-day matches he would make a big difference to our side. We would like to pick him as our fifth bowler, but he must prove to us first that he can be more consistent.

Frank Hayes played nine times for England and captained Lancashire from 1978 to 1980. When he retired on medical advice in May 1984, it was the bitter end to a brilliant career that had been plagued by a series of accidents, both big and small – a source of sadness for Lancashire's coach John Savage:

Frank was the most unlucky player I ever met. His bones were so brittle that he was always breaking fingers and thumbs. When he was injured, there were no half measures. I remember him dislocating his foot at Lord's and it ended up at right angles. It was a dreadful sight. The surgeon who saw it said it was a million to one chance, but it happened to Frank. All he did. was slip when turning for a run, but when you looked at the mess, you'd have thought he'd fallen off the pavilion roof.

He had some horrible injuries, but he was brave and kept battling back. What was so annoying with Frank was that at the start of a season he was usually the fittest fellow on the staff. He trained hard. He did a lot of running.

Some people doubted his temperament because he rarely did well when he played for England. The truth is, he only ever played against the West Indians. Against Daniel, Holding and Roberts in their prime, and even then he hit a hundred on his debut in 1973. I don't agree with people who say his temperament let him down. I saw nothing wrong with his confidence or his attitude to the game. He was a very fine player and very aggressive at times. I once saw him hit 34 in one over off Malcolm Nash, the Glamorgan bowler Gary Sobers hit for his famous six sixes.

No coach expresses greater confidence when looking to the future than Stewart Storey, who is certain that Sussex can build around a nucleus of homegrown players, especially David Standing, Allan Green, and the talented Wells brothers, Colin and Alan:

To my mind David Standing could be the next captain of Sussex. He is very mature. He has above-average ability and is gifted with a deep understanding of the game. He is just 20, yet he has already proved he has the application to become an outstanding county cricketer. As it happens, he went to the same Newhaven school as Colin and Alan Wells, so he's been well prepared.

I played in Colin's first game for us, and he looked a very good seam-bowler. Then, when I took over the second eleven, I watched him blossom out into a hard-hitting batsman. He reminds me of Ken Barrington. He loves to bludgeon the ball over mid-wicket.

Colin is dedicated and ambitious. At no time will you see him give his wicket away. If anything his bowling has interfered with his progress as a batsman. At one point in his career he lost confidence in hitting over the heads of fielders, which he does best. He ended up chipping the ball, like a golfer, and kept being caught. So we found a quiet corner and had a chat. Deep in my heart I knew that if he remained patient everything would click into place again. When Eastbourne Week came around he suddenly flourished with a series of big scores and since then he has never looked back.

His brother Alan joined us with Adrian Jones and David Smith. I had a hunch about him. He has the ability to bowl, but there is something lacking in his approach to his part of the game, though I have no desire to push him on it. Alan, like Colin, was coached by his father, and in a way they kept pad manufacturers in business. He taught them how to thrust their left leg down the wicket, which prevented the bat from reaching the ball. It took me months to get them out of this habit.

Alan has scored far more runs than I ever expected of him so early in his career. He has done well because of his determination. He is hungry for success. He is a tremendous outfielder and a terrific asset in the one-day game.

Allan Green is definitely the most gifted player we have. And that includes all the big names on our staff. He has the ability to play every shot in the book, and is a wonderful timer of the ball. What he lacks at the moment is the concentration to be a consistent run-getter.

In the second half of the 1981 season he scored seven hundred runs and we thought he had solved his problem. Then he lost his confidence and went out of the side – and scored a hundred in his first second-eleven match. Alan has this infuriating habit of making batting look so easy, and then suddenly he plays across the line and is back in the pavilion.

He is one of the best players of fast bowling I have seen. He gets right behind the line of the ball and his reactions are extremely sharp. He has enormous potential, but I have to keep giving him a kick up the backside just to get him motivated.

As an opener for us, Allan's skills have been a little lost in the shadow of Gehan Mendis, a fine attacking player, who has been here since 1971. Mendis was born in Sri Lanka, but has qualified to play for England, an honour that would please him more than anything else in the game. On his day he has the ability to take the best attack apart. He has a very keen eye and some marvellous shots. In 1983 he proved to me that he can play a long, responsible innings. What I want from him most of all is to produce runs on big occasions, something which he has not done for us yet.

The newest discovery among Yorkshire's galaxy of glittering gems is the young slow left-arm spinner Paul Booth, from Huddersfield. For a coach renowned for his careful comments on players, Doug Padgett is unusually open in his praise of this remarkable lad:

Paul first came here when he was fourteen. He just turned up at one of our schoolboy sessions at Headingley. For someone of that age he had an uncanny command of length and line. I had never seen anyone so young bowl so consistently. There is usually a great variation in length and line, especially with spinners.

He was so good that I asked him to bowl to our best batsmen in the afternoon. Then I went out to watch him playing for a League side. I followed him around. I was captivated. A short time later I went to Ray Illingworth and I said, 'Look, I think we ought to put his lad in our second team. Give him a go.'

He was a bit nervous at first. Maybe overawed. But the following season, as a sixteen-year-old, he came on leaps and bounds. He's a grand lad who wants to learn. He's very conscientious. The type who usually go to the top.

I didn't have to do a lot with him. I just taught him how to bowl to different players and to think a bit more. And I tried

33

to get him to bowl slightly more side-on. Little things – nothing drastic.

Of course, there is only one way to learn – out in the middle. A player can only go so far in the nets. You can't test temperament in there. We've had several players who looked great in the nets but have been disastrous in the middle. Then we've had players who've looked grim in the nets, but kept doing their stuff on the square. I have one now. If you saw him in the nets you'd pick holes in him left, right and centre. But he doesn't half score runs in the middle.

Simon Dennis and Paul Jarvis are the two young pacemen Padgett expects to spearhead Yorkshire's attack in the years to come:

Simon Dennis is a fast left-armer who swings the ball back from over the wicket. He pushes them across. He's a great fellow to have because there are not many of his type around. What he needs is experience. He's just twenty-three and still learning the job. Jarvis is in the same position. He's only nineteen and has a whole future ahead of him.

I remember sitting with Alec Bedser once and he told me how he used to bowl for hours, morning, noon and night, to Members at the Oval. He reckoned he was nearly thirty before he was in the top flight – before he knew where he was pitching every ball. Mike Hendrick told me the same. He was also thirty before he mastered the game.

Though generally pleased and optimistic about Yorkshire's bowling power, Padgett is far from satisfied with the progress of Graham Stevenson, who played in two Test matches for England between 1979 and 1981:

Graham ought to have given us more. He has not applied himself fully. We would like him to be more aggressive in his bowling. His ability is not in doubt, but it is being wasted at times because he doesn't concentrate hard enough. He could do far better for us.

He came up through me, and I always knew he had the ability to play for England. The pity is, he's played only twice. If he'd put his mind to it he could have played a lot more.

The tall, powerful Hugh Wilson looked one of Surrey's best bowling prospects for a long time, until suddenly he crashed from the scene almost as quickly as he arrived.

Speedy and aggressive, Wilson found the media writing him up as an England prospect almost before he had marked out his run. Then, having failed to fulfil his potential, Surrey released him in 1983 and he moved on to Somerset as part of cricket's growing transfer system that is developing more and more along football lines.

David Gibson: Hugh Wilson worked very hard to establish himself as a pace bowler with Surrey, but he didn't take enough wickets. The Press wrote him up as an England certainty long before he had a chance to show what he could do. Talent is one thing, character is another.

Before we released Hugh, we told him what he was doing wrong. We don't let players go without first giving them every chance to prove themselves. A lot of money is spent on bringing them through the system, so we don't throw them out before we are absolutely satisfied there is nothing we can do for them.

Few players in modern-day cricket have produced the stamina, skill and consistency of 'Deadly' Derek Underwood, a left-arm aggressor whose only concern has been to attack no matter how placid the pitch, how fierce the batsmen, or how weary his body.

Colin Page knew him from the start, and his tigerish zeal to do well every time he turned his arm over was evident from the very first game they played together, as Page recalls:

Someone dropped a catch off him at slip and he couldn't believe it. Then I dropped one. Derek got so upset I thought he was going to throw a tantrum.

'For goodness sake calm yourself down,' I said. 'We set high standards at Kent. No one goes around deliberately dropping catches.'

Naturally I realised his reaction was all part of his make-up. He wanted to take wickets. He wanted to do well. But he was young and exuberant. For his own good, I had to cool him down. I had to teach him how to control his emotions.

That was many years ago, of course, and we laugh about it

now. Derek is the gentleman of cricket. A super example to any player at any level. He's my favourite guy as a man.

Not every batsman who comes up to county standard, or even attains an England cap, is gifted with natural talent. There are those who reach the top by sheer hard work and determination, as Lancashire's forthright John Savage confirms:

Barry Wood and Graeme Fowler are just two of the many self-made players who spring to mind. Mediocre batsmen who worked hard and made themselves good players.

Fowler spent hours on his own, working at his game. He came to us at fifteen and played in our second team a year later. He was always at the nets. He couldn't get enough of batting.

Since he's become an England player, his technique has taken a lot of stick, especially for the way he's been edging catches outside the off stump. Well, perhaps he is a bit flash, but some batsmen are always vulnerable to certain shots. There's not a player living who doesn't have a weakness in one department or another.

Fowler runs into trouble when he's facing a right-arm over bowling across his body. All left-handers find this ball difficult to play. Some critics have made a great song and dance about it, but it's something that he can cure. We are hoping to eliminate the weakness by degrees, and in the meantime continue to concentrate on building up his strengths. He plays very straight and is very strong. At his best, Fowler is a delight to watch, though I suppose the good spinner will give him trouble from time to time. Above all else, he is brave, which is a vital factor today.

David Hughes has been another fine professional for us. Not a prima donna by any means. Players like David, the bread-and-butter men, are the people you need when times are hard.

Peter Roebuck is one of an increasing number of professional batsmen now wearing spectacles or contact-lenses and proving that a slight eye deficiency need not hamper a good player's progress even at the highest level. Geoff Boycott, Clive Lloyd, Mike Smith and Eddie Barlow have all worn spectacles at some time during their playing days. And Derek Aslett, Eldine Baptiste and Robin Dyer are among the new men coping with ease.

36

Peter Robinson says of Roebuck:

Peter first noticed his eyes were not quite right when he began to misjudge the ball in the field. Strangely enough, they didn't trouble him when batting, though he was wearing glasses when Andy Roberts struck him in the face. It was a terrible blow, but Peter has nerves of steel and his confidence remained solid. He plays quick bowling as well as anyone. He enjoys batting with Viv. It takes the pressure off him. Viv is usually into his stride in just two overs, which makes it a lot easier than when two batsmen are pushing and scratching for runs.

To be fair, I thought Peter would have scored more runs than he has done for us so far. If I had to be critical of him, I would say that he has overdone his on-side play. While at Cambridge, and even in our second team, he was freer to play his shots. He was more relaxed. But once he moved up to our first team, the pressure was on him to achieve results, particularly in the important one-day games. That's when he became more intense. That's when he went into his shell. I also noticed a lot of right hand coming into his play, but he worked hard to correct that and his form improved.

Peter showed potential at a very young age. He played for our second team when he was just fourteen.

Cricket seems to run in the Roebuck family. Peter's brother, Paul, is a fine player and has joined Gloucestershire. We wanted him to come here, but I think he was reluctant to follow in Peter's shadow.

I think Peter, and Vic Marks, too, benefited from playing university cricket. It brought them on quicker than if they were playing in our second eleven. By playing for Oxford and Cambridge they gained valuable experience.

Vic's career has changed a lot. He came to us as a batsman, and went in at number four for our second team, and bowled just a bit. Now it's very much the other way around. Our batting has always been so strong that he's hardly had a chance to stake a claim for a place higher up the order. He's even batted at number nine sometimes. Vic has worked hard at his bowling. As hard as Phil Slocombe worked at his batting.

Phil got bogged down with theory. He rather blinded himself with science. He kept changing his stance. When he started with us he was very much a front-foot driver. Then he thought he should improve his on-side play and became open-chested. He lost his strengths a little, and at the end of 1984 decided to retire from the first-class game.

A recent exodus of experienced players has left Worcestershire with a gigantic task of team-building over the next five years. Faced with this enormous problem, Basil d'Oliveira says:

We've had a lot of success in the past twenty years, though we've fallen away a little lately. One reason for this was losing so many senior players at the same time. Glenn Turner, Norman Gifford, Younis Ahmed and I all went in two seasons. That's a lot of experience, and it takes a long time to replace. A club needs a thriving youth policy to produce instant replacements, but we don't have the volume of young players in Worcestershire for that type of operation.

We are the smallest county in the championship. We are not a Kent or a Lancashire. So we look to people from outside the county, though we always keep a close eye on local lads who are showing promise. It is vitally important that we assemble a good first-team squad. That is our plan at the moment. It is very much a rushed job. We are desperate for players like David Humphries to come off. As a wicketkeeper he has an excellent pair of hands. One of the best in the business. But he drifts into terrible lapses of concentration. When David is on song, he is a big asset. So he must get his concentration right if he is to help us through.

Every year thousands upon thousands of young boys dream of becoming a county cricketer when their schooldays are over. Kent's likeable all-rounder Derek Aslett was one of that crowd and his coach Colin Page reckons that for outright dedication, no one in the game could have done more to achieve his ambition.
Colin Page: Derek has always been one of the quiet types, right from the first time I saw him when he was just thirteen. In those days his father would bring him all of fifty miles from Dover to Chatham every Saturday morning. They were always there when the doors opened at 8.30. Nothing kept them away – not even snow, ice or floods. To be honest, we were more interested in Derek's leg-spinners then. But he was so keen that his batting continued to improve. He has matured into a

confident, aggressive striker of the ball now and must eventually go into the top bracket.

Derek was quite different from Kevin Jarvis, for instance. When Kevin came to us he had very little obvious potential. But what he did have was absolute dedication and that more than anything else has made up for all his technical shortcomings. He has never known when to give up. And he has proved, yet again, that if a player has the right attitude just about anything can be achieved in the end.

Neil Fairbrother's cricket-mad parents were so convinced that their newly-born son was going to grow into a talented batsman that they named him Neil Harvey, after the brilliant Australian left-hander of the day. As it happened, Neil turned out to be a left-hander too, and his parents' confidence has been fully justified.
John Savage: Neil was thrown in at the deep end, yet he scored 94 in his first championship match.

He came here originally as a thirteen-year-old lad on an Easter coaching course. He had lunch, met the players, and thought it was great. Then we followed his progress.

Young Fairbrother's sporting skills have since extended on to the rugby field, though he takes care that this vigorous game in no way hampers his development as a cricketer. Once January comes he stops rugby altogether.
John Savage: Neil's contract with us applies only from April to September, so we cannot insist he should stop playing rugby earlier, but he is quietly advised to do so. We don't want any last-minute injuries to first-team players. It would be barmy for something to go wrong at that time of year, and especially when not even playing cricket.

We put Neil in our second team when he was only sixteen, but he didn't do much then, though we knew there was a great deal of ability inside him waiting to burst out. It eventually came at the Cambridge Festival, where he had a superb week in our Under-19 side, and when he came back I asked him what plans he had for the future.

No matter how well a lad might do for us, we always encourage our seventeen and eighteen-year-olds to get the best education first. To pass their exams. But Neil wanted to take a crack at the game, so we signed him on a two-year contract, which is the biggest we ever give anyone.

Fairbrother, along with Paul Allott, Steve O'Shaughnessy and wicketkeeper John Stanworth all enjoy a game of golf, and I think it's good for them. It helps them to relax. After all, Dexter, Graveney and Arthur Milton were all mad keen about golf and it never affected the way they batted.

Following David Lloyd's unexpected departure to league cricket in 1984, Lancashire surprised many by going south to Worcestershire, where they successfully prised away Alan Ormrod from an opener's post he had held for twenty-two years. Worcestershire coach Basil d'Oliveira has the highest respect for Ormrod's fine technique:

This chap is still one of the best players of fast bowling in England, and he's been blessed with a marvellous temperament. When he opened with Glenn Turner, it was Alan who took the brunt of the quick bowling, though Glenn helped Alan, too.

Their styles were very different. While Glenn was able to get the ball away, Alan could stick around all day. They complemented each other. All of a sudden we would be 60 for no wicket, and Glenn would be on 43.

Alan probably played in the shadow of Glenn and one or two other great players. He often didn't get the credit he deserved. In all the years he played with us, I never saw him hook, cut or pull. And if someone slung in a bouncer, he simply ignored it. He just ducked – he couldn't be tempted.

Peter Willey's parting with Northamptonshire was hardly an earth-shattering shock, though few would have expected Leicestershire, known for their youth policy, to be heading the queue for his signature.

Ken Higgs: When we heard through the grapevine that he wasn't happy at Northants we decided he was too good a cricketer for someone else to sign. We thought of him as the ideal man to replace Brian Davison, who was leaving to play in Tasmania.

Somerset's rise as the one-day giants has brought much pleasure to a county that struggled for years to give their members something real to shout about, though an intoxicated few have occasionally carried their celebrations a bit too far.

Peter Robinson, however, also remembers the bad old days when the committee worried not so much about where the next win was coming from, but more about where they could raise the money to stay in the game. Robinson recalls those depressing times:

I remember 1969 in particular. That's when Brian Close came to us. We were a poor side then, and the committee in their wisdom decided we should have more experienced players and went out and signed three youngsters – Close, Cartwright and Jim Parks. Dad's Army, really.

Tom was 36, Close was 38, and Parks was about the same age. Close took over as captain, Tom was still a fine bowler, and Parks was keeping wicket well. We also signed Derek Taylor from Surrey and Allan Jones, the pace bowler, from Sussex.

Our finances were so bad that we were sharing second-eleven matches with Gloucestershire, picking six lads from each county.

Peter Denning and Brian Rose came to us at that time and jumped straight from schoolboy cricket into the county championship. They came up too quickly. We were in the lifeboats then. We had started to sink in 1968, and by 1969 we were going under fast. Brian and Peter were thrown in at the deep end.

Rose and Denning remained together until 1984 when Denning retired from the first-class game.
Peter Robinson: Peter and Brian helped to keep us going in the early Seventies. They were a tremendous opening combination, especially in one-day games.

With the steady demise of Denning and Rose, and the inconsistent Phil Slocombe still struggling to make an impact, Somerset have searched hard to find a regular opening partner for Peter Roebuck. For a time, Jeremy Lloyds looked the most likely to solve their problem, and Robinson recalls how Lloyds came to Somerset:

Jeremy had been around for many years before he came to us. After leaving the Lord's groundstaff he played a great deal of second eleven cricket for Glamorgan, Hampshire and Worcestershire. All along I felt he had ability, but he would

41

rattle up a magnificent twenty or thirty and then throw the lot away.

He came to me one day and asked if there was a chance of coming on the staff. I thought he was worth a try, so I put his name forward to Roy Kerslake, who was chairman at the time. Money was tight then, but I said to Jeremy that we could offer him £500 to the end of the season.

'Oh, no', he said. 'I've had another offer. Can I sleep on it?'

'All right,' I said, 'but that's the best I can do for you.'

To be honest, there was probably a bit of kidology on both sides.

Anyway, next morning my telephone rang and Jeremy said, 'I'll come. I'll take the £500.'

I assured him that if he worked hard, the opportunities were there for him. I told him the only way to make people sit up and take notice was to score hundreds. And he did. He battled his way through.

He put in a lot of effort and we capped him in 1979. He has made himself into a player. He has taught himself how to build an innings. All I could do was talk to him. Force him to concentrate and keep going. Convince him that committee people only remember big scores. He must have listened because one day he went with our second team to Ebbw Vale and hit 262 off Glamorgan, the county who not long before had let him go. (*Towards the end of 1984, Somerset released Lloyds and he moved on to Gloucestershire.*)

2

Captains, umpires and pitches

Few would disagree that as a captain Mike Brearley had that special gift of making himself look cool and in full control even when things were going badly. He never seemed hurried, worried, or caught in two minds. He demoralised many merely by his laconic air of assurance and his knack of making the right decisions time and time again.

But now Don Bennett, coach and colleague at Middlesex, reveals that away from the spotlight, Brearley was far from being the confident, imperious demagogue that he appeared on the pitch.

As chief coach, Don Bennett worked closely with Brearley for more than ten years. It was Bennett who produced the goods for Brearley to show in the shop window. The very structure of their jobs meant that clashes of policy, and even of personality, were unavoidable as the years went by. While Brearley demanded instant success, and almost at all costs, Bennett had to seek out opportunities to blood his best young players, the stars of the future.

Don Bennett: He was undoubtedly the best captain I ever saw. People will now obviously compare Mike Gatting with him, but that will be unfair. They will be forgetting that Brearley had four years of learning to be captain in our side before he was anything like successful. That was his period of grounding.

Nevertheless, he learnt quickly. He was always sounding people out – always bouncing ideas around. He spoke to players like Radley, Emburey and whoever was keeping wicket. He picked their brains. It was always discuss, discuss, discuss. Always bringing players in. Then he made his judgement. Bradman did it the same way. And he became terribly annoyed when people agreed with him too easily. He had a strong personality, and when someone is that powerful and also has a remarkable record of making the correct decisions, it can be difficult for people to disagree with him.

Yet he was not infallible, and he knew it. He knew that he had to be kept on his toes. And for that reason alone he expected those around him to speak up and say what they thought. He became very cross one day after we had gone into a match with only two spinners on a pitch that turned square. He demanded to know why no-one else on the selection committee had thought of playing a third spinner. Of course, there can only be one boss in a cricket club and he was certainly that here.

The problem with Brearley was that as soon as he became successful he wanted more success. He was impatient. His mind worked largely for the present, while I thought more of the future. He couldn't afford to look two to three years ahead. That was my concern. The more successful we became, the more difficult it was for me to push the young ones forward, and because of that our opinions didn't always coincide.

In the final moment of reckoning I am a firm believer that the captain is the boss, so if things go wrong on the field it is he who should carry the can.

Many outsiders probably got the impression that Brearley was always cool, calm and collected. He was nothing of the sort. He could get quite steamed up when people upset him. To his credit, if he wanted to slate someone, he always did it in the privacy of the dressing-room. Never in the open. I admired him for that.

The finest compliment any cricketer can receive is when a member of the opposition praises him as the best of his kind in the game. Surrey's former coach David Gibson refers to Brearley as 'probably the best captain in modern times.' And he not only extols his skills as a communicator, motivator and psychologist, but makes the practical point of how he controlled matches with positive decisions on the field:

You can always tell a good captain by the way he reads the game and handles his bowlers. A good team with a poor captain will be hard-pressed to win a title of any sort. There are some players who couldn't captain a school Under-13 side when they are thirty years of age.

For a long time Middlesex had a good team of individuals

but achieved nothing. Then Mike Brearley came along and they started to pick up trophies.

I remember the day Surrey played Middlesex in a Gillette Final at Lord's and he kept moving his fielders around before each new batsman had time to reach the bottom step. He blocked off the batsman's favourite shots. He put fielders in the right places. He stopped the runs. It was brilliant tactical stuff.

The best captains do their homework. They gather information about the strengths and weaknesses of opposing players. Brearley's brain worked three times faster than the average captain's.

A good skipper is like an outstanding batsman or bowler. He's a specialist. The man who tilts the balance between winning and losing. A good captain gets the best out of his players. He doesn't allow them merely to bat and bowl. He pushes them to the limit.

Of course the world's best captains have made their mark in many differing ways. Not all have been masterminds. Some have coaxed and persuaded. Others have manipulated. A few have even bullied their players into making an impact.

The Reverend David Sheppard fell into the 'persuasive' category. Alan Oakman, now of Warwickshire, remembers him well, especially for the way he steered England and Sussex to many great triumphs:

Playing under The Rev. was a great thrill. He always wanted to win, though I am sure, to this day, that it was the Sussex players who finally drove him into the Church. He had a marvellous sense of humour – until something went wrong. The Rev. was definitely the best captain I ever played alongside. Though not a natural cricketer, he was dedicated to the limit – and a fine batsman.

He led by example. He placed himself close to the bat and made his pressure felt. He was the only captain I ever played under who wrote and thanked me for what I had done during the season.

On many occasions, after running around and picking up the ball, I would see him standing in the middle, applauding what I had done. He's the only captain I have ever seen doing that. He had the knack of making players feel important.

In 1956 the England selectors thought I was good enough for two Test matches against the Australians and I played at Headingley and Old Trafford.

During that famous Old Trafford Test, The Rev. was fielding in the bat-pad area for Laker when he suddenly went up to our captain Peter May and said that as he hadn't played cricket for some time he felt his reflexes were not sharp enough for that position. Yet he had only just hit a hundred off such magnificent bowlers as Lindwall, Miller and Ian Johnson. His reflexes were in great shape! So May asked me if I would go in close. I had fielded in that position for Robin Marlar at Sussex, so May knew I had some idea of what was required. Thanks to Laker's superb bowling, I took five catches.

Marlar took over as skipper when The Rev. went into the Church, but after a short reign he was succeeded by Ted Dexter, who was a real extrovert and loved to entertain.

Though Sheppard's obvious grace and charm impressed Oakman so much, he still places Mike Smith, of England and Warwickshire, as joint top in his captains' popularity poll:

Mike Smith was good for us, even if he was a bit eccentric and extremely forgetful. He mixed well with the players, both on and off the field. That was his secret. He got the best out of everyone because he was so eccentric.

He used to call our West Indian all-rounder Bill Bourne 'Chocolate Drop'. Because it was Mike, he got away with it. No-one else would have.

And his awful absent-mindedness almost left us a man short one morning. He had promised to give Jack Bannister a lift to the ground, but when Mike arrived there was no sign of Jack. About thirty minutes later we saw Jack hurrying across the playing area. He was carrying his bag, and as he panted up the steps he shouted out to Mike, 'Why didn't you stop?'

'Stop! Stop! Where?' asked Mike.

'I stood in the road and you almost knocked me down,' said Jack.

Oakman's admiration for Mike Smith is generously endorsed by Ken Higgs:

46

He was very shrewd – the best I played under. He knew that when players reached Test standard, he didn't have to boss them around. He didn't tell them how and where to bowl. He let them get on with their job. And he got the best from them.

Ray Illingworth was the same. He was always thinking and talking about the game. In my experience, though, batsmen have usually made the best captains. I have seen so many bowlers deliberately put themselves on to improve their figures when the later batsmen come in.

Cyril Washbrook was a very hard skipper. He thought no one else could play cricket but himself. If some of today's professionals had played under Washbrook, they'd have trembled in their socks. He was in charge. He was the major. If he put you in a position on the field and you wandered just half a yard, he would know. And he'd roast you for it in front of the lot.

For all that, he commanded respect. He mixed with the team in the evenings and chatted freely, but he still gave the feeling that you shouldn't dare cross him. He played it hard. He would turn up at a game and say, 'Right, there is no reason why we shouldn't beat this lot in two days.' And if we believed in him, we did it.

These days a lot of players like to slip away and sleep in the afternoons while their side is batting. They come off the field and snooze until it is their turn to pad up. Cyril Washbrook would have shaken them up. They wouldn't have yawned, let alone slept. The whole object of cricket is to learn from watching. He insisted everyone was outside to see every delivery.

Leadership is so important. Look at Yorkshire. They've had a great bunch of lads for the past six to eight years, but the team has not done half as well as its potential.

I know a lot of those players personally. I don't know precisely what has gone wrong because I am not in the camp, but they have not produced the goods as a team. And now they don't even have a fast bowler.

What bothers Ken Higgs most about present-day cricket is the way so many three-day matches are allowed to die on their feet:
It is soul-destroying when you see your opponents settling

for one slip and a Sunday League field after bowling only twenty overs. The whole object of the game is to bowl the other side out.

I sat with Warwickshire's manager David Brown one day and after about twenty overs his side had one slip and the rest spread wide in the deep. So I asked him what he had in mind. He said, 'We don't have the people to bowl you out.' How, in the name of the game, are they going to find bowlers if they don't give them a chance? There is nothing more disheartening to a bowler than to get an edge and have no slips to take the catch. Any team in the world can bowl to a Sunday League field with everyone deep on the boundary.

Then we played Middlesex, and they deliberately declared with eight wickets down, just to stop us from getting a bonus point. We won the match in the end, but what they did was unnecessary.

To hell with bonus points, that's my attitude. I believe all points should be awarded for a win. In that way sides would have to bowl each other out. That was the case in my playing days. But captaincy methods have obviously changed a lot since then.

Basil d'Oliveira agrees . . . Cricket is crying out for a more positive approach. The three-day game in particular. Once a captain sees that his side can't win, he puts up the shutters. He strangles the game. We desperately need more sensible declarations.

Unless there was a fight on, I could never play. If I went in for Worcester or England and the score was something like 350 for two, you could bet your last pound that I wouldn't stay. But 50 for six . . . now that was different. That was a challenge.

I remember playing for England in Australia and going out to face their off-spinner Ashley Mallett. We had a very big score and I took a mighty whack at his first ball and was caught in the deep.

Ray Illingworth came in next, and as we passed each other he gave me a long, cold stare.

As it happened a friend of mine was sitting with Sir Donald Bradman and he said to the great man, 'That was a lousy shot'.

'Oh, no', said Bradman, 'that was a good shot. It was positive.'

D'Oliveira's aggressive attitude was superbly emulated by his fellow-South African Eddie Barlow, who revitalised Derbyshire in his three magnificent years as captain of the club. Phillip Russell recalls how Barlow lifted them from the doldrums.

Until he came here we were rightly known as a negative, defensive side. But Eddie changed all that. As captain, he taught us to be positive. He was a tremendous motivator. And when he left we probably went backwards slightly.

Though Eddie wore glasses, they never bothered him as a batsman. If anything he used them as a tactical ploy to slow the game down when things weren't going right for us. He would take them off and wipe them after every ball.

Eddie was clever. He understood men. He knew how they thought. He had a lot of wonderful ideas, but the club wasn't ready for him.

We had no facilities to capitalise on reaching the Benson and Hedges Final in 1978. We had also won seven championship matches, but we had no real home base to make any money. Times were so bad that we didn't have a bar on any ground. We had a tent, but the money from that went to the caterers. We had a small, loyal membership of about 1,400. That's all. So we couldn't build on our success. And the same happened when we won the NatWest in 1981. That was a tragedy, because Eddie had brought positive thinking into the club. Both in the game and off the field.

When Eddie left, David Steele came in. On reflection, he was probably not the right man. I found him a super chap, a good clubman, a fine batsman, and an under-estimated left-arm spinner. But he worked so hard at his own game that he didn't have the time to motivate the other players. He relied on people being like himself.

Eddie was different. He knew he was a very good player, and if something went wrong with his own game he would give himself an hour to put it right and then concentrate fully on motivating the others.

Steele stayed only three seasons with Derbyshire before returning to Northamptonshire, where his benefit in 1975 had yielded £25,000.

With Steele leaving, Derbyshire were left to search frantically for a captain who could command the respect achieved by Barlow and continue in office for a respectable length of time.

During a traumatic 1983, several of the club's senior professionals declined the job, and it was left to young Kim Barnett to set an example and attempt to weld the team together again. He was only twenty-two, and many feared the extra load would affect his own personal contribution with bat and ball, but he enjoyed a fine season, topping the batting averages, and accumulating 1,423 runs – to the delight of Phil Russell:

That was the one thing that bothered the committee. But I think the captaincy has improved Kim's play. We could so easily have gone for Geoff Miller to be on the safe side. Personally, I never saw it as a gamble. I had seen Kim do the job beautifully in the second team and for the Under-25s. He's got a quick cricket brain. He's got strength and flair, and he is a very powerful character.

It hasn't always been straightforward for him. He's had to sort a few things out, and he's done it a bit at a time. Given the luck, I think he'll play for England. He definitely has the talent.

We've had more captains in the past seven years than any other first-class county, but we are fairly well settled now. I don't think there is any specific reason for us having so many captaincy problems in the past. We've had administration changes, and changes in the playing staff, and when things go wrong in a club it is usually the captain who gets the knocks.

To be honest, I think some of them found the pressure too great when we lost an important game or two, and then decided to relinquish the job. Twenty years ago a captain wasn't under the same type of pressure to get results, so he would have lasted much longer.

Unlike Barlow's huge success with Derbyshire, overseas captains have done little to inspire Glamorgan. The Pakistanis Majid Khan and Javed Miandad both had a spell as captain, without ever registering a glimmer of hope, which hardly surprised those who understood the prodigious difference in culture and the obvious language barrier, especially with Miandad who has struggled to communicate in English, let alone in Welsh.

Kevin Lyons: I suppose we've changed captains in the way some people change shirts. After Wilf Wooller left we seemed to have a new skipper every season. Tony Lewis was technically effective, but he had a good side under him. Then we had Ossie Wheatley, Majid, Robin Hobbs, Barry Lloyd, Javed, Malcolm Nash, Alan Jones, Mike Selvey, Rodney Ontong and Uncle Tom Cobbley and all.

Swapping captains at that rate was bound to unsettle the side. We have cried out for good leadership but we've not often seen it. Ossie Wheatley did a fine job. He had a great rapport with the players. Mike Selvey also impressed us. Coming on from Middlesex, where he had a lot of success, he made our lads aware of competing. He had a mental hardness about him. He led from the front.

Selvey left Glamorgan suddenly in August 1984, with eighteen months of his three-year contract still to run. His reduced pace had brought him only 25 wickets at an average of 39.80, and his retirement came just ten days after being left out of the team, though his reason for leaving was given officially as a recurring knee injury. Rodney Ontong then took over, becoming Glamorgan's eighth captain in eight years.

Of the first captain he played under at Glamorgan, Kevin Lyons says:

Wilf Wooller was captain here when I played in my first few second-team games. He was a big man – both physically and in the way he acted. I thought he was a brutal captain, though I knew he meant well.

One year Glamorgan were so short of an opening batsman that Wooller said he'd do the job. He ended up battered and bruised, but he collected some runs as well. No one could accuse him of not leading from the front.

Another captain of that era who led by example was Freddie Brown. At forty-five, Brown was still driving Northamptonshire forward with his own special brand of infectious enthusiasm, as chief coach Brian Reynolds remembers:

He was a remarkable man. I admired him immensely because he never asked anyone to do what he couldn't do himself.

I remember playing against Glamorgan at Ebbw Vale and

we were a seam bowler short. So Freddie opened with outswingers, turned to off-spinners in the afternoon, and then came back with leg-breaks later in the day – at the age of forty-five. And all he wanted for lunch was a gin-and-tonic to keep him going. Freddie was a very astute captain. He studied the opposing players. He never missed a trick.

Neither does Keith Fletcher, according to his Essex coach and colleague Ray East, who has nothing but praise for his brisk, impish skipper:

Technically, Fletch knows the game inside out. He is the best captain I have played under or against. He is extremely observant. He can relate the strengths and weaknesses of practically every player in the game. If you can't get a batsman out, ask Fletch, that's what I say.

Everyone admires him because he is such an attacking captain. He is always applying pressure, and leads by example. He always fields close in, a few yards from the bat, and he promoted himself to number three in the batting order to tackle the quick bowlers.

He even uses his spinners as attacking bowlers. I remember we were playing an important one-day match against Somerset and Richards and Botham were batting. Fletch took the ball and threw it to me. I thought he was mad, putting a spinner on against two such aggressive batsmen. But he was right. In no time at all I had bagged them both. Then he took the ball off me and I didn't bowl again. I never asked him what was going through his mind, but it underlined his skill as a thinking captain.

He is always attacking. He wants to win and is prepared to lose. He is willing to make a game of it with his declarations, which can't be said of everyone.

Personally, I thought England treated him shabbily after their tour of India. Leading a side in that part of the world must be the hardest job in cricket, but all he got for it was the sack.

Off the field, Keith tends to be quiet and reserved. Some people say they find him difficult to get to know. But there's nothing cold or aloof about him. We've been close friends for many years and I know he's someone I can trust. I enjoy being in his company.

When Ian Botham arrived in Somerset, he was looked upon to some extent as the natural successor to Brian Close, both of them being charismatic, belligerent, brave in the extreme, and both having a total disregard for status, dogma or the opposition.

Senior coach Peter Robinson speaks frankly about Close. Their relationship, in fact, was far from harmonious, which makes his sprinkled praise even more noteworthy. As a left-arm spinner, Robinson launched his career with Worcestershire, but on finding four other identical bowlers at the club decided to transfer his skills to Somerset, where he soon came face to face with the abrasive Close:

I played under Brian's captaincy, and I found that he treated everyone in the same way – which wasn't always good. If you weren't the type of player who could take his stick, and fight back, he could get on top of you.

I had played under Colin Atkinson and Brian Langford, so I found Close a bit overpowering. Under him I lost confidence in my bowling. I went to pieces. In two seasons I went from bowling 250 overs a season to bowling just twenty. I seemed to freeze. That's the type of pressure he put on me. I would hold the ball in my hand and couldn't let it go. I literally struggled to pitch it down the other end. It wasn't that people had hit me around. I just felt under pressure. My confidence had gone. In truth I needed help and encouragement, but Close wasn't the type to give it to me.

One of my last games was in a Gillette Cup-tie at Leicester. It was probably the most amazing match I ever played in. We won the toss, and I opened the innings with Mervyn Kitchen. We put on between sixty and seventy before Mervyn was out. Then Close came in. Ray Illingworth and Jack Birkenshaw were bowling and the wicket was taking a bit of spin. Being a left-hander, it wasn't easy for me to get the ball away. Within a minute of Close coming to the wicket, he walked up to me and said, 'Come on, lad, you've got to get on with it. You've let these spinners pin you down.'

The only way I could get a run was to lap a bit. To turn the ball off my legs and scamper through for a single. Close played a few good shots and we moved on nicely. A big score looked possible. Then disaster struck us. Illingworth called up Ken Higgs to bowl his seamers from the Old Pavilion End. Close was facing, and Higgs went round the wicket to him. Close pushed the first two back, but when the third ball went down he took the biggest swipe of all time and his middle stump was knocked flat to the ground.

I can see umpire Jack Crapp now . . . 'That's it, gentlemen,' he said. 'That's lunch.' And off we trooped.

When I reached the dressing-room everyone else had slipped away to eat, so only Close and I were there. And he looked across at me and said, 'Do you know, lad, your running between the wickets is diabolical!'

Those were his first words.

'And another thing,' he said. 'Why the hell didn't you tell me it was a one o'clock lunch?'

There was no mention of the terrible shot he had played.

I was wearing a tattered old pair of batting gloves and as he went on talking he said, 'Are they the only pair you have?'

'They are actually,' I said. So he delved in his bag and pulled out a brand-new pair of Slazenger gloves and he threw them across to me and said, 'Use those'.

He was a strange chap, but I must say he did some tremendous work for Somerset during his six years here.

Anyway, we ended up with about 212, which we all thought was a good score. I had grafted on for 67 of them.

When we went out to field, A.A. Jones soon removed two or three and we had Leicester struggling at 50 for 6. Game, set and match, we thought. But Chris Balderstone was still there, and he and his partner kept picking up their ones and twos.

I remember Leicester had reached 120 when Mervyn Kitchen came across and said, 'We'll lose this one'.

'How the hell can we do that?' I said.

In the next over Brian Langford tossed one up to Balderstone who tried to sweep, got a big top edge and the ball flew high towards A.A. Jones out on the boundary. To get under the ball 'Jona' had to run about twenty yards along the boundary edge, and he not only dropped the ball but kicked it over the rope for four.

Then wicketkeeper Jim Parks took a bang on his thumb and had to go off. So Close stepped in.

'I've kept in a Test match,' he said, without thinking to ask whether anyone else could do the job.

So he padded up and took the gloves. And all the time Leicester's innings kept ticking along. Ken Higgs had come in and he kept pushing his pad down the wicket. So Close decided to bring back A.A. Jones to blast out the last few.

Trouble was, he didn't bowl straight. Then Close complained that the gloves were too small. So he took them off and he stood there, trying to keep wicket to A.A. Jones with no gloves on, and the ball was flying all over the place. He stopped some, dropped some, and the byes kept mounting up.

In the end Leicester beat us. I think their committee had gone home at tea, disgusted with their score of 50 for 6. We felt it was like knocking someone down for fourteen rounds and then losing in the fifteenth. To be honest, Close lost control. He seemed to think that Leicester had to score fours to win, but they did it comfortably with ones and twos.

On another occasion that season I batted with Close in a John Player match at Edgbaston. He had scored about 70 when I went up to him and said, 'If you keep going, Brian, you can score a hundred here today.' Next thing, he took a huge slog and was out, caught. I finished up with 71 not out, and when I got back to the dressing-room he was there waiting for me, and said, 'If you hadn't mentioned that hundred I wouldn't have been out.'

I couldn't believe my ears. . . .

Even with his uniquely powerful, if volatile, leadership, Close failed to raise Somerset to a level where they could compete effectively with the bigger guns.

This pleasure was still a few years away, waiting patiently for the placid, almost introverted leadership of Brian Rose, whose success was especially gratifying considering Somerset were ready to boot him out after just one year on the staff.

Peter Robinson: The committee almost got rid of him soon after he came in 1969. They virtually said, 'We don't think you are good enough for county cricket.' So he left and went off to college to train as a teacher. Then he came back in 1972 and proved them hopelessly wrong with a magnificent 125 against Kent, and convinced us all that he would be here for a very long time.

Brian developed into a natural captain. His one-day

leadership was supreme, especially with his bowling changes. He always got the best out of Joel Garner.

People have said that Brian took over a good side, but he still had to lead it. He still had to make important decisions on how best to use all the wonderful talent he had around him. At times it can be more difficult to lead when you have so many good players than if you had no worthwhile players at all.

Though Brian was very, very sound, he would be the first to agree that his three-day captaincy was not exactly in the Mike Brearley class. Brian tended to let county matches drift to a finish. Perhaps having so much one-day success made us all a little complacent when playing our three-day games. We didn't have the right attitude.

There were times when an important Sunday match was coming up, and on the Saturday the captain and his players would be thinking 'We must win tomorrow. . . .' We were not thinking about the game in hand. That's why our three-day performances suffered.

Late in his career, Brian had trouble with his eyes which forced him to wear glasses. The problem came at the worst possible time. He was playing his best cricket and had just been picked for England. The trouble eventually corrected itself, which was so important to him because he's essentially an 'eye' player. He puts in a superb round of golf.

Peter Sainsbury: Skippering a county cricket team is the most difficult job in sport. I have seen many honest people try and fail. And many clever people, too.

I can remember one match in particular when I tried it. Butch White was the player involved. He was a close friend of mine, and a fine bowler. We had shared a room for eight years while we travelled with Hampshire.

Over those years I had watched him bowl his heart out for skipper after skipper. He was the type who would bowl twenty overs non-stop in the heat of the afternoon and still come back and give his lot in the last fifteen minutes of the day. Butch was a captain's dream. But, could he do it for me? Never.

One thing is certain, bowlers in general don't make for good captains. I remember skippering our second team at a time when we were trying someone different every week. I was also the chief county coach and on this particular day we were giving a trial to a young West Indian who was pretty fast.

As usual I stood at short-leg, and at the end of the lad's second over our wicketkeeper came up and said that he liked the way the boy bowled but felt he was falling away a bit in his action.

Because I was so close to the stumps my eyes had been riveted on the batsman. I hadn't noticed what my bowler was doing wrong. So now I decided to watch his next delivery.

I watched him run up, leap, land, release the ball – and then felt a sudden thud in my chest. The batsman had played a bad shot and I had missed a simple, straightforward catch.

Nick Pocock did well as captain until he retired. He might not have been the greatest batsman in the world, but he knew how to talk to people.

We gave him a year's trial when we were looking for someone to replace Bob Stephenson, and I was so impressed that I recommended he should do the job permanently.

Pocock remained captain until August 1984, when he stunned the committee by saying he didn't want to play in the first team again. Mark Nicholas was then appointed and at twenty-six became the second youngest captain in county cricket.

Peter Sainsbury's respect for Pocock is echoed in equal measure by Stewart Storey's unequivocal admiration for John Barclay, a county player since 1970 and skipper since 1981. The Sussex coach says of his leader:

John Barclay and I work closely together. He is a very sympathetic man. He eats, sleeps and drinks the game. He is so generous he gives everyone a chance to perform to their best – even to the detriment of his own game. That is his main failing. He always puts others before himself.

In a three-day game he will usually bowl Chris Waller first. But in a one-day match he will always put himself on first. And he is positive. But he belittles his own performances.

He is a good batsman and a good bowler and one of the best captains I have ever seen. He gets tremendous respect and support from his players, and he is an excellent judge of a game and its outcome. As a batsman he has struggled at times. He has lacked assurance. He has the potential and ability to do much better and I have spent hours trying to boost his confidence with the bat.

My experience has taught me never to appoint a captain who is a bowler. It's the road to disaster. When you are a bowler it is an enormous responsibility to decide when you should go on and come off, and who to put on next.

When it comes to controlling batsmen like Viv Richards, and to tactics in general, it's the captain who plays the major part. Choosing the right man for captain is extremely important. It can make all the difference between success and failure.

Most of Yorkshire's recent problems have surrounded the choice of skipper. People like Chris Old, Neil Hartley, Geoff Boycott and David Bairstow have all tested their qualities of leadership and initiative. Chief coach Doug Padgett:

A captain must always be able to put the team's interests before any personal situation. He must be able to persuade some and bully others. He must command respect and be able to communicate.

Then, if he can do all that, he must be able to size up a game. Be able to read it better than most. And then finally back his judgement with spirit and determination.

Caught in a good philosophical mood, Graham Wiltshire of Gloucestershire says:

Captaincy is the only feature of cricket that cannot be improved by coaching. You can look at people and you will know at a glance the ones who can be natural leaders. It works in the way it does for finding officers in the Army. Someone just fits the bill.

Though Mike Procter captained Gloucestershire for a time, I think every county should be led by an Englishman, or in Glamorgan's case, by a Welshman.

It doesn't always follow that senior players make the best captains, though a few years in the game should help. A good captain will need to learn his trade. Just like a bowler or a batsman, or even a coach.

Colin Page goes even further: Skippers are born. No-one can coach or manufacture a leader. He just shines through. Stuart

Surridge was one of the truly great captains. He was surrounded by immense individual talent, yet he had the skill and character to weld them together into one of the greatest sides ever to play championship cricket.

He had exceptional players under his command, like Laker, Lock, the Bedser twins, McIntyre, Constable and so on. Yet when Surridge shouted they all came together. He won their respect. He was a wonderful disciplinarian.

Mike Brearley was another gifted leader. And Asif Iqbal was a highly intelligent captain. An outstanding tactician. Players of this calibre are a rare breed. Ray Illingworth was one of them, and now that he has retired he would be the ideal person to manage the England team.

Just as captains stand alone, exposed to vital decisions and instant judgements, umpires remain even more vulnerable to pressure. No one understands their predicament better than the county coach, and it is encouraging to note that they all emphatically applaud the stand being taken by our umpires against the ever-increasing number of aggressive players who are sometimes more concerned with intimidation than dismissing opponents through skill and fair play.

Ken Higgs: Umpires are going through hell now. This bat-pad business is terrible. Players are shouting for catches when they know the ball is nowhere near the bat. I suppose players have cheated since the game began, but it's never been as bad as it is now.

I shall always remember an incident at a Roses match when a certain Yorkshire batsman was caught behind. A ball from Brian Statham nipped back, gloved the batsman and went through to the wicketkeeper, but the umpire was unsighted.

Brian appealed, but the batsman stood his ground. Geoff Pullar was fielding at slip and at the end of the over the umpire said to him, 'Did that fellow do me?'

Geoff looked him straight in the eye and said, 'I have no comment to make.'

That was enough. The umpire knew the batsman had stuffed him.

By next morning we had all chatted about this incident. We knew full well that the umpire was less than pleased with the batsman, so we decided that if the ball struck him on the pads anywhere near the wicket we should throw up our arms and let out a real noisy appeal.

It took just five minutes to get rid of him – lbw. Whether that amounted to cheating the umpire, I don't know. But as time went on that fellow got a terrible reputation for being a batsman who didn't walk.

In those days the umpire usually gave the batsman the benefit of any doubt. So that man was stupid. He cut his own throat.

I can think of nothing more foolish in cricket than trying to con umpires. They talk among themselves and anyone who deliberately deceives them goes down as a marked man.

Batsmen are standing their ground now far more than I can ever remember. For my sins, I walked every time. Being a bowler, I was annoyed when batsmen hung around when I knew I had broken through.

I am sure this practice has become more common because of the big money at stake. But it's still down to the player's conscience. And it's no good saying this or that chap doesn't walk if people in your own side are doing exactly the same. The onus is on the captains.

It is only when you see the standard of umpiring in other countries that you can fully appreciate the quality of the people doing the job here.

I remember a Test match in the West Indies when the Chinese umpire Sang Hue gave Gary Sobers out lbw for nought. The place broke into a riot. Bottles and bricks were thrown on the pitch and we had to run for our lives. And all because an umpire had the courage to do his job. Sobers was plum in front, but Sang Hue was probably the only umpire on the island who would have given him out for nought. It was a frightening experience. And though the noise eventually died down we couldn't play for the rest of the day.

Also I shall never forget the time England went one up in the series and we moved on to Trinidad to play the final Test. Before the match even started one of the umpires was told that his house would be burned down and his wife and children killed if he gave a 'bad' decision. They were saying the West Indies had to win or else. The umpire then announced that it would be his last match because the risks were too great for him and his family. That's the type of pressure they face in the West Indies.

Alan Oakman is equally forthright:

In my day batsmen were brought up to walk. We didn't need an umpire's finger to tell us that we had touched the ball. There was more honesty in the game then.

Now the cheating has taken over, and I hate it. At Warwickshire we take great care to stress to our players not to get involved.

When I went on the umpires' list my card was marked immediately. I was told there were three players to look out for in particular. They always waited for the umpire's decision.

From my experience most umpires have good memories. If you stuff them once, they will stuff you good and proper in the end.

Peter Robinson remembers having no hesitation in giving himself out, caught at the wicket, when just three short of his maiden hundred – rather than cheat the umpire:

We were playing Middlesex at Lord's and I was on 89 at close of play. I was awake all night. I kept thinking that I just needed to collect a few singles next morning and I'd be there.

Everything went well until I reached 97. Then John Price bowled me a terrible ball. It was short and wide and it had 101 written all over it. So I swung the bat, got the tiniest tickle, and the ball smacked into John Murray's gloves. I waited for the appeal. But Price said nothing, and Murray said nothing. In fact, Price was about to walk back to his mark when Ron Hooker suddenly piped up at short leg. 'Howzat,' he said. Without even looking up I turned and walked off. And I was just three short of my first hundred.

John Langridge was the umpire, and he came up to me at lunch and said, 'Thanks very much for what you did. I could never have given you out.'

In those days we tried to help umpires. Too many players stand and stare now. They won't budge until the umpire has raised his finger and given them out.

Brian Reynolds: My blood boils when I see batsmen hanging around. Only when there is real doubt should they wait for the umpire's decision.

Colin Page doesn't mince his words, either. Any batsman who deliberately stands his ground goes down as a 'cheat' in Page's book:

If a batsman knows he has snicked the ball and the wicket-keeper catches it, that batsman should walk. He wouldn't hang around if he were caught in the covers.

Players who are always appealing also get under my skin. I am disgusted by what I hear now. It started in Test matches and has worked its way down. Even schoolboys are doing it.

There is deliberate intimidation, and it puts the umpire in a terrible position. Counties and captains, in particular, have a responsibility to see that it is stamped out.

Don Bennett, however, is far less severe on the subject:

As I see it, British players are the only ones who walk, anyway. If you think about it, all those who walk must be on a loser. After the war several English batsmen needed more than a gentle push to get them back to the pavilion.

I remember a young batsman getting a rollicking from Bill Edrich for not walking when he knew he had snicked the ball. Turning to Jack Hearn, who was chief coach at the time, Bill said, 'That's right, isn't it, Jack?'

To which Jack replied: 'Not likely. I've never walked in my life.'

'Neither did I,' said Patsy Hendren. And Gubby Allen also told me that he always waited for the umpire to give him out.

Meanwhile John Savage believes that limited-over games have placed excessive demands on an umpire's concentration:

They have so much to watch for in one-day matches. They must count the overs, check the white discs, see no one is standing inside the circle, add the bowler's overs, and still watch for wides, no-balls and all the other many important split-second decisions that are down to them alone.

Umpires have never had it so hard. There are four or five major competitions now, and each with a different set of rules.

That's why we tell our players that if they hit the ball we

expect them to walk. Every effort should be made to take the strain off umpires, not to put more on.

Given the chance to amend the game's existing laws, Kevin Lyons would like to see all appeals limited to the bowler and wicketkeeper. Nor is that the only change he would make:

I would also like to see the lbw law changed entirely, to allow a bowler to get a decision even if the ball pitches outside the leg stump.

The new wave of appealing also bothers Basil d'Oliveira:

I feel sorry for umpires. They work under tremendous pressure and are being intimidated. I don't mind players appealing, but it's the way they appeal, with their arms shooting up, and glaring at the umpires, that infuriates me.

Ray East sympathises: Like all of us, umpires must have a mental blank from time to time. They will make mistakes. Just like batsmen and bowlers make mistakes. It's part of the game.

It's part of being human. Yet many players and the public, too, seem to think our umpires should be right every time. I suppose those who feel that way should try standing in the middle for six hours on a scorching day and see how well they can concentrate. It is only then that they will realise what type of pressure our umpires work under and how errors are inevitable.

Meanwhile Brian Reynolds is both firm and amusing when talking about the role and ability of British umpires. He says:

This country should take it upon itself to educate umpires all over the world. We definitely have the best. Australian umpires in particular are quite mediocre, and that's being kind to them.

On the lighter side of umpiring, I always bring up the name of Alec Skelding, who had terrible eyesight. He wore thick, pebble-lens spectacles and before he put his white coat on every morning he would come into our dressing-room and go straight to the washbasin down the far end. Then he'd take an eyeglass from his pocket, pour in the Optrex, and give his eyes a good wash before going out on the field.

One morning the whole team stood and watched him going

through his routine. Then he put on his spectacles, turned round, tripped over a bag on the floor, and fell flat on his face.

Alec's eyes were so bad that he relied entirely on sound for giving people out caught at the wicket.

I remember we played Gloucester at Northampton and Freddie Brown was our captain. Halfway through the morning Alec glanced up at the sky and said, 'Skipper, once that dark cloud comes over the sun we shall be going off for bad light.' Freddie looked at him daft. It was a glorious day. The light was perfect and, apart from that one small cloud, the sky was a beautiful blue as far as the eye could see.

Eventually the cloud did drift over the sun and Alec said, 'Right, that's it.' And he picked up the bails and walked towards the pavilion. But the cloud was so small we didn't have time to reach the boundary rope before the sun was shining again. So Alec turned round and led us back to the middle. His eyes were that bad.

But Alec was no cheat. He was very kind. A great character, and we all loved him.

There was a certain warmth and respect between players and umpires in those days. The way some players appeal now is a disgrace to the game. Only the bowler and wicketkeeper should be allowed to appeal for lbw decisions. It's absurd when players at square-leg and third-man join in. Umpires in my day wouldn't have tolerated those antics. Frank Chester would have been furious.

Batsmen who stand their ground when they know they've snicked a catch put terrific pressure on umpires. Batsmen should have the good grace to walk. That's the way I played it, and that's what I expect from our lads.

Concern for the treatment of umpires is more than matched these days by the anxious glances cast at our first-class pitches that tend to come in all sorts of colour, pace and bounce.
David Gibson: Bad pitches have helped to make the game more frightening. Good groundsmen are a dying breed. Nine-to-five groundsmen will prepare nine-to-five pitches. Surrey are lucky. We have Harold Brind, who is a perfectionist. One of the old school.

Peter Robinson is even more forthright:

Wickets have lost their fire. I am convinced that's why this country doesn't produce genuine fast bowlers. The wickets are puddings. Lifeless. How often do you see the ball fizz through and rattle into the wicketkeeper's gloves? In the West Indies the ball is always hopping and darting around. In Gordon Prosser at Taunton we probably have the best groundsman in England, though our luck hasn't always been this good.

The bad wickets of my day were terrible. I remember one year at Bath when the council thought we were looking after the pitch and we thought they were. In all the confusion no one supervised it. So, just a fortnight before our match with Worcestershire, a committee man turned up and almost collapsed in shock. The grass was up to his ankles and we had to cut it with a scythe. Then we ran a mower over it, and rolled it gently.

Cecil Buttle was our Taunton groundsman then, and he went up to Bath and smothered the wicket in marle. From out on the boundary, it looked good, but once the first ball pitched, great clouds of dust blew all over the square.

Fred Rumsey took eight wickets in the first innings and Bill Alley took eight in the second. We had a lead of forty – and won by an innings! It was ridiculous, considering Worcestershire had a star line-up that included Kenyon, Headley, Graveney, Richardson, Horton and d'Oliveira. The game was over in a day and a half. Of course, we don't have wickets like that now.

Taunton was a lot better. Cecil Buttle used to swear by worms. Now every ground has killed them off. Wickets have been swamped in Surrey loam. Layers and layers have been coated on like Plasticine. No wonder pitches are so dead. At Taunton we were delighted because Gordon has struggled to restore some life and all his hard work is beginning to pay off.

Basil d'Oliveira puts much of the blame on those groundsmen who deliberately doctor wickets, either to suit the home side's bowlers or to take the zip out of the opposition.

Pitches are definitely getting worse. The ball is coming through lower and slower. Trouble is too many groundsmen are preparing wickets to suit their bowlers. I suppose it must go down as a form of cheating.

Nottinghamshire, in particular, have been accused of cutting wickets at Trent Bridge specifically to suit their pacemen Hadlee and Rice, though manager Ken Taylor is quick to dismiss these claims:

When we won the championship in 1980, certain newspapers and some television people gave us hell. They said we had deliberately prepared our wickets to suit Hadlee and Rice. It was a load of baloney and it took away the gloss. I still feel very strongly about what was said.

That was the year our groundsman Ron Allsop gained top marks from the umpires for the one-day games, and came second in the three-day games. His wickets were tip-top.

No one here will deny that our pitches were quicker and did bounce. But our players batted on it. And Mike Brearley scored a magnificent century here when Middlesex beat us.

Strangely enough, no one in the game complained. It all came from outside. The truth was that Clive Rice and Richard Hadlee were bowling magnificently. And Eddie Hemmings took ninety wickets with his off-spin. I also remember we bowled Warwickshire out for 49 at Edgbaston, which proved we could do the same no matter where we played.

I think one or two of our wickets did go wrong over the following season because we were trying to prepare faster pitches. I think we went too far. We just didn't get it right.

People criticise groundsmen without thinking of the difficulties they work under. Just imagine trying to prepare a square during the weather we get in December, January and February. Anything can happen. It's not an exact science at all.

For county cricket I am one of those who believes a wicket should always slightly favour the bowler. Any bowler. Spinners like to bowl on quick wickets too, because if the ball gets bounce there is more chance of batsmen getting nicks and being caught. On the flat pitches we see so much of now, a bowler can find the edge and the ball won't even reach the wicketkeeper.

3

Quick bowling

Colin Page was sitting in his car at the Dartford cricket ground when a tap on the window disturbed him. He looked out and saw a blond-haired boy trying to speak to him through the glass.

The lad was no more than twelve, and he had deliberately picked out Page, the chief coach to Kent County Club, to ask a question that was playing on his mind.

'Please, Mr Page', he said. 'Can you tell me how I can become a county cricketer?'

Page opened the door and asked, 'What's your name, then?'

'Graham Dilley,' came the reply.

Page was impressed by the lad's attitude and good manners.

'Ask your father to write to me,' he said.

It was just the encouragement young Dilley needed. Dilley senior wrote that night, and young Graham was invited to Page's indoor school at Chatham, where he became a regular every Saturday morning.

Page recalls those raw, early days:

Graham looked a much better batsman than a bowler, but once we launched him as a bowler everything changed. He had a dream action. Since then, I'm afraid, he's been bombarded with advice and become terribly confused. He was so bad during the early Eighties that he didn't know what to do next. His confidence was ruined.

For a bowler, Graham has two big advantages. He is always beautifully relaxed and he has such a magnificent build. But a career that should have been long and distinguished has suffered because too many people have tried to tell him what to do. Too many players have been destroyed by people meddling from the outside, and I've seen my fair share of them. . . .

Hard work and dedication are fixations with the indefatigable Ken Higgs, who is quick to praise those who show effort, but caustic about those who don't strive hard enough to get the best out of their potential.

Of pace bowler Alan Ward, who played for England five times between 1969 and 1976, and joined Leicestershire from Derbyshire, he says:

Alan was one of the fittest players I ever met. But he baffled us. Our captain Ray Illingworth wanted to bowl him in four-over spells, which would suit anyone. I would play until I was ninety doing that. But Alan couldn't do it. I suppose some bowlers don't have very big hearts. If things don't go right for them, they tend to pack up. Because of this we couldn't go on playing him match after match. Many times I sat and talked to him and tried to gee him up. But some days he wouldn't perform at all.

I remember one match in particular. He had just returned from injury and he was playing for our second team at Grace Road. Barry Duddleston was captain, and between them they set an attacking field of four slips, two gullys, and a leg slip. There were only two players in front of the bat. Then Alan ran in and the ball bounced twice before it reached the batsman. And this was a bowler who had played Test cricket!

He was a strange chap. He worked hard in the nets, but to get him to do his best on the field was practically impossible. For some reason he rarely played for us against his old county Derbyshire – which was odd, because we thought he would relish the chance to prove that they were wrong to let him go.

We thought there might be something psychologically wrong, but no one could say precisely what. Alan was one of those bowlers who was full of beans one day and down in the dumps the next. We never knew what he was going to be like.

We played at Lord's one day and he bowled quicker than I had seen anyone bowl for a very long time. He broke Mike Brearley's hand, so that must have impressed the England captain.

Then we went down to Kent and he bowled like a drain. It was quite unbelievable. He wasn't the same person. There was no apparent reason for it, unless he had fallen out of the wrong side of the bed.

Yet for all his peculiarities, he had the potential to be a permanent England bowler and could have been playing now. Instead, the last I heard of him he was keeping a public-house in Derbyshire.

A mischievous smile spread across Stewart Storey's face as he produced a real controversial gem, and he was deadly serious about it. He said:

I have come to the conclusion that the thicker you are the better your chances of becoming a good quick bowler. The least you think of your problems the better you will perform.

Just remember, a quick bowler has a run-up of thirty yards, the sweat is pouring down his face, the sun is blinding hot at seventy degrees, he's in his tenth over, he's not taken a wicket, three catches have been dropped and the soles of his feet are red raw and sticking to his socks. And still he must struggle on and churn it out.

An intelligent boy would probably look up and say, 'What the hell am I doing here? Why me? There must be more to life than this.'

I don't think there are enough quick bowlers coming through from our schools. The standard of pitches are poor, and the masters don't help. If a boy runs up and bowls quickly, but sprays the ball around a little, the master will be so scared someone is going to be hurt that he will ask the lad to slow down. All they think about is length and line, and that's where the big mistake is made. The lad will see this as a chance to go easy.

'This is a doddle,' he will say. And from that moment on he is finished as a quick bowler. He will never recover his speed and natural rhythm. I much prefer to see a young chap who bowls all over the place, but is genuinely fast, because I know I can do something with him.

Adrian Jones is a good example of this. He's home-produced and has enormous potential, but in his first winter with us he bowled in the nets and kept hitting the rigging on both sides. I thought, 'What the hell have I done in taking him on?'

Then I taught him how to grip the ball properly and started to smooth him out. He responded well and bowled for our

69

Young Cricketers for three seasons. He does everything automatically now.

Fast bowling is the bane of every coach's life, and like most quick bowlers Adrian is being plagued by injuries. He's already had the lot – ankles, toes, calves, back and both shoulders. It's terribly depressing for him, and for everyone else at the club, particularly now that he's made his way into the first team.

Quick bowler Jonathan Agnew is a player who Leicestershire have always hoped would fulfil his potential and thus silence the critics who keep writing him off as overrated.

His rejuvenated form in 1984 finally convinced the selectors that he deserved his chance, and he represented England in one Test against the West Indies and another against Sri Lanka, though each time he bowled only moderately well. Ken Higgs says of him:

The worst thing possible happened to Jonathan. When he came here he played under Ray Illingworth, who classed him as a Test prospect, and said so. Now the fact that someone says a player has Test potential doesn't automatically mean that he becomes one. He has to work hard and keep producing good performances. Jon has finally got down to doing that and now, five years on, he has become a genuine Test contender.

And why are good fast bowlers such a rarity in England? Nottinghamshire manager Ken Taylor puts forward an original and plausible reason:

I am not a scientific person, but I believe it's all due to the motor-car. We ride about in them from the word go. Getting out of a car, your back aches. You have to straighten yourself. I am certain this has something to do with the shortage of good quick bowlers and with all the injuries they suffer.

At one time quick bowlers came out of the pits in cageloads. Even that supply has dried up. Miners no longer work in the same way. They used to develop enormous back muscles, but the jobs they did are mostly done by machines now.

Richard Hadlee is always feeling the physical strain. There's not an ounce of fat on him. He's built like a pipe-cleaner. He does so well because of his beautiful action. It's all rhythm. He couldn't bowl like Fred Trueman or anyone like that. He's so different from Clive Rice. At one end it is all muscle and strength, and at the other we have Richard.

Leicestershire's Les Taylor is someone who literally left the pits to test his talent as a county bowler.

Ken Higgs: He is very strong and he's learnt to bowl properly. In his early days he bowled so wide of the crease I couldn't believe it. All he did was slant the ball across to the leg stump. But once he saw that the ball could be moved around, he demanded to know how it was done.

Of course there was no way he could swing the ball unless he bowled closer to the stumps, and I preached and preached that to him. I suppose I helped him a lot. I showed him what to do in little ways, and every bit counts in the end.

Strangely enough, I could always get him to bowl side-on in the nets, and the ball would swing like a banana. But we found there was a big difference when he bowled off two paces indoors compared with his full run in the middle. So he had to work hard.

He felt he couldn't get side-on because he had to run off the wicket. Now he gets much farther across with his front foot, and he moves the ball away, as well.

All I regret about Les Taylor is that he went to South Africa and got himself banned from Test cricket. To some extent he went on the rebound. I know that he was disappointed about not going to India with the MCC, but that was just unfortunate. If he had been patient I know his chance would have come eventually. When the South African offer was first put to him, he virtually told me he would not accept it. But it was obviously an attractive carrot, and the more he looked at it, the more tempting it became. We must remember that Les Taylor was a lad straight out of the mines. He was presented with a substantial financial offer, and he had his wife and family to think about.

Alongside Willis, I am sure he would have made a big difference to England's attack. I am sorry he never gave himself the chance. Now he may never know how good he might have been.

That emotive subject of bouncers is another topic on which Higgs has firm views:

71

I was brought up when batsmen could hook or knew how to duck and sway. Reg Simpson was the best. Sling a bouncer down at him and he'd move his head a couple of inches either way and the ball would go whizzing by. He was never hit. Never even rushed. And the bouncers are no quicker now than they were then. A bouncer should never get a batsman out.

For a while there was a rule in county cricket which allowed a bowler just one bouncer an over. It could never last. If it happened to be the first ball of an over, the batsmen were on the front foot for the next five.

Then, when they went into a Test match, they got a bouncer every other ball and found they couldn't cope. So batsmen must learn to combat it, but if they don't hook, they shouldn't try to. They should get out of the way and let the ball go past.

Not many young batsmen hook. They duck. But it's different when facing someone like Joel Garner. He bowls a good-length ball in your rib-cage all the time, but the number of occasions I've seen batsmen duck against him is unreal.

At Leicester we have a good young bowler in Gordon Parsons. Sometimes he pitches the ball up beautifully, and it swings. Yet when he's played with Andy Roberts and Les Taylor, and seen them bowl bouncers, he's thought he should be doing the same. And he's been hit out of the ground.

For some peculiar reason he once tried to bounce Ian Botham with the second ball of his first over and the ball finished up in Millington Road.

The umpire then turned to Gordon and said, 'That's all for this over.'

And Botham called down the wicket 'Don't worry. At that pace he can bowl them all day.'

Like Botham, the belligerent d'Oliveira also relished the short ball.

To me, the bouncer was like a red rag to a bull, and you can't coach the shot to combat it. You can't tell someone, 'We're desperate for runs, go out and hook.'

The National Cricket Association are talking about teaching it now. It has always been an instinctive shot. You either play it or you don't. There are no half-measures. Given the option, I should like to see it coached, preferably with tennis balls. They hurt less if they hit you on the head!

Tennis balls should be used more often in coaching. They bounce better. When the ball bounces, the batsman can play more shots. Cricket balls tend to keep low and can make life difficult for lads of eleven to thirteen.

I learnt all my cricket with tennis balls. I grew up in a block of flats in Cape Town. The entrance had six steps and the bowler would stand at the top and throw tennis balls down at me. That's where I learnt to bat. The ball would bounce all over the place. Then, in later years, when I played on the Cape Town matting wickets, I found the ball was always up around my neck and I could cope with it. That's why bouncers have never bothered me.

Graham Wiltshire reckons that with so much coaching taking place now, the number nines, tens and elevens are all trying to play like ones, twos and threes, but don't have the ability:

So they push forward and back, occupy the crease, and use up time. They frustrate the opposition, particularly the quick bowlers.

When batsmen started to do this, one or two overseas gentlemen had just come on the scene who were not strictly members of the Fast Bowlers' Union. So the bouncers crept in, and then they became the norm. And the helmets arrived.

Many years ago I remember George Emmett saying to me that if I tried to bowl bouncer after bouncer it meant that I was not good enough to remove the batsman in the normal way.

I was brought up when fast bowlers used the bouncer as a shock ball, just as the leg-spinner used the googly. It was a tactical ploy. Not a weapon. Short-pitched balls deliberately aimed at the head should be barred from the game.

Cricket has a reputation for being a contest of skill and strategy. I fail to see the skill in slamming a bouncer down, ball after ball.

A glut of costly no-balls rather than bouncers highlighted Derek Pringle's problems in a difficult time in 1983 when his inconsistent run-up threatened to destroy his international career, and even put his county job in jeopardy. Essex coach Ray East is sure that the trouble started when Pringle toured Australia with England:

All of a sudden we found that Derek was bowling eleven-ball overs for us, and I honestly believe it all started because he didn't work hard enough.

Along with our other coaches Graham Saville and Bob Richards, I asked Derek to come to the nets where we could look at him closely. The first thing we did was to put a yellow disc near the bowling crease, so that he had something positive on which to focus as he approached the wicket. The idea worked well, because all through those practice sessions he didn't bowl a single no-ball, though we all realised it was not quite the same as bowling in a match. Still, the trick seemed to work and his run-up was generally all right from then on.

At that time he liked to enjoy himself a bit, but later on he worked hard at his game and within a season or so he was back playing for England again. The turning-point came when he went to Australia for the winter and stayed with Geoff Lawson. This seemed to change his whole attitude to the game.

Gladstone Small was another no-ball sufferer, and he too hit his bad patch shortly after being put on standby for England, in 1982.

In one match, against Middlesex, umpire Bill Alley called him eleven times in one over. Including a wide, the over lasted eighteen balls, and Small had to finish it by bowling off a five-yard run.

After that worrying performance Warwickshire had no alternative but to drop him and send him back to the nets to examine every movement in detail.

Alan Oakman: When Gladstone had marked out his run, David Brown, Neal Abberley and I made him close his eyes, so that he kept his head up and wouldn't be looking for the crease to place his feet. Then we took up positions to study his action. Neal watched him leave his mark, David stood halfway along, and I was at the wicket to see where his front foot came down.

We all noticed that his rhythm changed from ball to ball. There was no consistency about his run-up. On occasions he was as much as six inches out in his delivery stride. Instead of bowling, and then following through with a smooth action, he was hesitating, and then overstretching.

We cured this problem quickly enough, but then Gladstone pulled a muscle and was out for five weeks. When he came back he broke down again, so little was seen of him in 1983. He bowled just 110 overs and took ten wickets.

A long rest did him a power of good and we are now confident that he has the fire and pace to impress the England selectors again.

Small is one of many bowlers who started life as a spinner and switched to pace almost by chance.

His name came up when Warwickshire suddenly went short of a quickie for their Under-19 side and Rex Warbank, a schoolmaster, suggested they should try Small, 'a spinner who can slip in a fast one.' And he did so well for them that Warwickshire signed him there and then.

Full of praise for fast bowlers, Oakman says:

They work very hard. A batsman's life is a doddle compared with all the work fast bowlers have to do. When quick bowlers see batsmen playing airy-fairy shots, slip fielders dropping catches, or the ball flying over the stumps, it's no wonder they become so volatile. If they didn't, they would be useless. Fast bowlers must have fire in their belly to have any chance of making an impact.

Bob Willis came back to the dressing-room absolutely drained after a day in the field. He bowled his heart out. And he was not helped by his action, which was hardly perfect. It put enormous strain on his body.

Norman Graham never reached the high pinnacles scaled by so many of his distinguished Kent colleagues, but his performances and professional dedication endeared him to everyone at the club and gave coach Colin Page, in particular, enormous pleasure and ultimate vindication.

Page explains:

Norman Graham was a bit special. When he was turned out of Birmingham University he came to us for a trial, and I was so impressed I signed him on a three-year contract.

Then a few weeks later he played in our second team at Taunton, and he bowled so badly that Les Ames, our manager at that time, came to me and said, 'Colin, you've wasted three years' good money on that fellow. He won't make a bowler as long as he lives.'

Norman's trouble was that he wanted to bowl too fast, and he wasn't built for the job. It was then that I remembered how he had bowled at the indoor nets when I first saw him. Because he was restricted for space in there he had to bowl off a short run and that steadied him. Bearing that in mind, I decided to reduce his run and to slow his delivery approach altogether. And I concentrated on getting him to take full advantage of his enormous height.

Norman stood 6ft 7in. He was as tall as Joel Garner and he bowled like him. He could bring the ball down from a tremendous height and cause all sorts of trouble.

In his thirteen years at Kent he gave us terrific service. Our supporters loved him. He took his benefit in 1977 and set a county record with £38,000.

Norman wore size 14½ in cricket boots which a Northampton cobbler made for him out of kangaroo skin. Three pairs usually lasted him about two years.

There can be no coach living who is more fanatical about practice than Ken Higgs, who explains that it all goes back to his early days at Lancashire and a strict policy at nets where bowlers never batted, and batsmen never bowled.

Recalling those raw and fascinating days, he says:

Brian Statham was a big help to me then. I learnt just by watching him. When you field at slip to a bowler of Brian's class you can't fail to improve. Brian was a cool customer. He had immense self-discipline, and by watching him I learnt how to control my feelings. If a lad beats the bat today, he usually throws up his arms and everyone goes around kissing each other. Not Brian. If he missed the bat and the bloke was nowhere near the ball, he just turned round and walked back to his mark.

Brian worked on percentages. If he bowled five good deliveries out of six, he knew he had to take wickets. That was his theory and I've yet to hear a better one. Any young lad who wants to improve his game should go out and watch the masters at work and learn by imitation.

Then I went to Australia and found that England's three

other quick bowlers, David Larter, David Brown and Jeff Jones, all had more speed than I could muster. I struggled a bit and my line was bad. I tended to bowl middle-and-leg and the Australians are renowned for their skill on the leg side.

So I knuckled down and thought hard about my game. I went to the nets and bowled at great players like Cowdrey, Boycott and Barrington. I set an imaginary field and bowled at their off stump. Thanks to this practice, my line improved.

When I came home from that tour I knew I had learnt to bowl the away-swinger. Then, during the following summer, I played in a Test match, and Brian Statham, who watched it on television, couldn't believe that I was bowling so close to the stumps.

My short time in Australia taught me that I had no chance of blasting out with my pace, and that if I wanted to take wickets I had to swing the ball to beat them.

The hard job I find today is trying to convince a young bowler, who is not particularly quick, of the value of being able to swing the ball. Lads seem afraid of being hammered in front of the wicket. They want four or five slips, whereas I wanted a mid-off. I invited batsmen to drive, knowing that if they were beaten by the swing they might get a snick. And if they drove me, I had a mid-off in position to nullify the shot.

Don Bennett was coaching his two lads in a net at the Middlesex indoor school when a fifteen-year-old lad called Norman Cowans walked in on a cold Sunday morning and asked if he could join in.

Don Bennett remembers it well:
I said to him, 'Come on then, let's see what you can do.' And he bowled to me personally. Even then his run-up impressed me. He had a beautiful smooth action, but best of all he was very supple. To my mind that is the most important feature in a fast bowler.

Our Neil Williams is the same. He's another coloured lad with tremendous potential. Our scorer Harry Sharp recommended him to us. Harry coaches at our indoor nets in winter and saw Neil bowling with London Schools and liked him.

Simon Hughes makes up our trio of home-bred pace bowlers. To be honest, I think all three will play for England in time. Mike Brearley rates Hughes very highly. Several counties have asked us about him, but I keep telling them he's not available.

People are always asking me why England can't produce good quick bowlers like they do in the West Indies and Australia. The truth is I think the English approach to fast bowling is all wrong and the West Indians have it right.

When we signed Wayne Daniel, I remember talking to the great Clyde Walcott who told me, 'Always let your lads bowl fast. Don't ask them to slow down.'

When I first see a quick bowler I always look for speed and a good action. But the action comes second. I never reject a quick bowler because his action might be poor.

In England we seem obsessed with wanting to change our fast bowlers. We mess about with their run-up, alter their action, adjust their grip. . . . instead of letting them get on with their job of bowling fast.

One of the most difficult West Indian bowlers to play against these days is Colin Croft. He's far from poetry in motion, but he's effective. He takes wickets. And that's what cricket is all about. No prizes are handed out for beautiful run-ups. But Croft is no faster than Graham Dilley, which makes me wonder how more effective Dilley would have been if left to bowl naturally.

Quick bowlers usually start to lose their pace once they reach the age of thirty. Trueman, Lindwall and Lillee all started to slow down at that point. But none of them suffered from lack of wickets. What they lost in speed they more than made up with extra control, swing, and change of pace, the three most important skills that go to making a world-class bowler.

Peter Robinson reckons there is another reason for the dearth of good fast bowlers:

I regret to say it, but quick bowlers in England tend to be a bit lazy. They don't like hard work. They can't blame bad wickets for everything. Sometimes it's the bowler who is at fault.

I keep telling our chaps that bowlers are the slaves of the game. It's the batsmen who get all the praise.

Arthur Wellard was a great all-rounder for Somerset, but I rarely hear people talking of his marvellous bowling achievements. They remember all his huge sixes, but they've forgotten that he took seven wickets for us match after match.

The biggest change by far in all types of cricket in the past ten to twenty years has been the daunting decline of spin bowling.

Don Bennett says, nostalgically:

In the Sixties it was all finger-spin and wrist-spin. A batsman was laughing if he could play spin. Quick bowlers were rarely, if ever, seen. A skipper would say, 'Toss one up, let's see if he can play spin.' Today he says, 'Make one bounce, let's see if he's chicken.'

Batsmen must have courage now. In certain circumstances bravery is more important than technique. Cricket is not for the faint-hearted, though I think there is far too much short-pitched rubbish bowled today. Spectators have no wish to spend a whole afternoon watching bouncer after bouncer flying over the heads of batsmen. It's a bore. The occasional shock ball might be all right, but to dig them in time and time again is an absolute crowd killer.

Reg Simpson was supreme against quick bowling. If the ball bounced, he swayed. He never tried to make contact with the bat. He wore bowlers down. He let them waste their energy.

Players like Botham and Gatting prefer to take the quick men on. Both are fine hookers. It's a reflex shot. If it's part of a batsman's armoury, then that's fine. But if it is not, then it's best to remember Reg Simpson, and sway.

To play fast bowling these days a batsman must be good on the backfoot. It's a major advantage.

Typically outspoken, David Gibson says:

People often ask me what I look for in a bowler. More than anything else I want to know if he is a wicket-taker. It doesn't matter whether he bowls off the wrong foot or has a rotten action. 'Does the lad take wickets?' That's always my first question.

4

Helmets, bats and the bowling machine

The wearing of helmets by batsmen and close-in fielders continues to stimulate argument wherever cricket is played, and a wide division still exists about their need, safety value, and where they stand within the laws of the game.

England's top eighteen coaches are far from unanimous on any of these points, and even the medical men are in doubt about the true protective strength of the average helmet following tests by the British Standards Institute in 1984.

On studying the results of those tests, an expert on head protection at the Institute of Aviation Medicine said:

'These helmets are practically useless. They do not offer proper protection against the risk of brain damage. The material inside these helmets, designed to absorb shock, is totally inadequate. The necessary alterations would not cost much, no more than 20p a helmet.'

The tests at BSI showed that when exposed to a force equivalent to a cricket ball travelling at 57 mph – considerably slower than the 80 mph of Malcolm Marshall and other West Indian bowlers – the helmet's fibreglass suffered damage, and the rigid head-form to which it was strapped began to dent.

It was emphasised that the tests were not a true impression of what happens on a cricket field when a batsman is usually struck a glancing blow and his head recoils. 'Even so, tests show that helmets in their present form are far from satisfactory,' said a spokesman for BSI.

Understandably, one major manufacturer reacted sharply, saying: 'We haven't had any complaints. The BSI tests are far too rigorous. No cricket ball strikes a rigid helmet and bounces back.'

So where do our county coaches stand on this contentious subject? Colin Page is in no doubt:

Helmets can save lives. That's as good a reason for wearing

one as any. They should be worn at all levels against quick bowling. Even during school matches.

There seems a good opportunity here for someone to start manufacturing helmets on a cheap line for boys between eleven and fifteen years of age.

But I am positively against fielders wearing helmets close to the bat. That's having an advantage over the batsman. If a player won't stand close without a helmet, then he should not be allowed to stand there while wearing one. This is intimidation and we need a TCCB rule to stop it.

Basil d'Oliveira: Helmets were a long way off when I played. I never wore one. In fact I never wore a cap. But cricket has changed since then and helmets are an essential part of the game now. Any form of protective gear must be good if it makes someone play better.

Just imagine the Americans playing cricket. They would be smothered under chest-pads and everything else they could lay their hands on. Which is sensible to me. What is the point in getting hurt if you can avoid it? If someone is going to be a better entertainer, a better performer, through wearing protective gear, then he should use it.

I honestly believe it was the helmet that gave Glenn Turner a new lease of life. He was hit a few times. Bernard Julian struck him in the eye and cut him badly, and he wasn't the same player for a few weeks. He drifted in and out – slipped away from the ball. But the helmet gave him confidence. It worked even for a player of that class.

Just look at all the protective equipment players have worn up till now. If they put their hands at their sides, everything is protected below the waist. So what is the sense of facing a ferocious bowler on a bad wicket without a helmet? Can you imagine a batsman going in without pads or a box?

The number of injuries we've had at Worcester of batsmen hit on the head or in the face is unreal. Richard Hadlee hit my son Damian on the head one day and only the helmet saved him.

Ken Higgs, however, holds a different point of view:
As I see it, all the helmet does is give batsmen a false sense of security. If the ball is pitched short, their first reaction is to

duck and they take their eyes off it. If they do that, they deserve to be hit. They get no sympathy from me.

I was always taught that the object of batting was to watch every ball. And no matter whether you were good or bad at it, you made certain to get out of the way of anything nasty.

My lads have been hit, and I've said to them 'What are your eyes for?'

I am seeing more and more English players now who start to push forward on the front foot, see the ball is about to pitch short, and turn their heads.

All right, so the helmet gives them some protection, but it doesn't alter the fact that they are not watching the ball. We are now having the ridiculous sight of helmets being knocked off from the back of the head. I remember Michael Holding digging one in against Barry Duddleston whose first reaction was to duck. He got so low that when the ball struck him on the back of the helmet he was almost out lbw.

The bounce varies so much these days that it is more important than ever for a batsman to keep his eyes on the ball. But I am not saying that helmets should be banned, because somewhere along the line a player could be killed without one.

Roland Butcher came perilously close to a terrible injury in 1983 when struck by Leicestershire's George Ferris. Middlesex coach Don Bennett recalls the incident:

Roland came off with three broken bones near his right eye and his eye muscles were badly damaged. It took three months of treatment to get everything working properly again.

We always knew he would need time to recover physically, and a little longer to recover mentally. He paced himself well. He coached with us at Middlesex, and with Don Wilson at Lord's, and had the occasional net himself. Then he went to India to play in a series of matches to complete his rehabilitation. It was a long process of restoring confidence.

Though he was wearing a helmet, the visor was not on, yet it's anyone's guess whether that would have saved him.

My advice is, if a helmet helps your confidence, then wear one. No one asks if a player should wear a box, yet it's potentially far more dangerous to be hit on the head.

The same principle should apply to fielders who wear

helmets in suicide positions. If you banned them, someone could get killed, and I hate to think what compensation complications would follow such a tragedy.

Having said that, I do believe some fielders are going in too close.

In every civilian job where the slightest degree of danger exists, the law insists that workers should wear some form of protective clothing. So why not in cricket?

Of course, the helmet first appeared in earnest when a number of overseas bowlers came on the scene and started to push their weight around, though Doug Padgett won't accept that the current batch of West Indian pacemen are any faster than the people he faced:

I know I haven't batted against Holding or Marshall or bowlers like them, but I'd be surprised if they were any quicker and harder to play against than Wes Hall or Charlie Griffith.

When I played, the bowler's front foot was allowed to drop well over the front line. Now the rules don't permit that. Today's bowlers are something like twelve to eighteen inches farther back when they release the ball, so I fail to see how a batsman has less time to play his shots.

What has changed are the extra number of bouncers. That's why we have helmets. I never wore one because they were only just coming in when I finished the game. To be honest, I don't think I would have felt comfortable in one. But if a helmet gives a batsman confidence then who am I to object?

Like most batsmen, I had my share of knocks. Charlie Griffith felled me with a frightening bouncer at Middlesbrough. I think he hit everyone that year.

What I am against are fielders who wear helmets close to the wicket. It's an unfair advantage. Players who normally turned their heads are standing firm and taking bat-pad catches because they feel safe in the helmet. That's not fair.

Derbyshire coach Phil Russell fielded in one, but it didn't do him much good, as he explains:

I had stood in the bat-pad position for six years and was hit on the head so many times that I thought 'Right, I'll let someone else do the job now.'

Then helmets came in, and I was at Chesterfield one

morning when Harry Cartwright was doing the bat-pad job for us. After three overs, Harry went off the field and Eddie Barlow said, 'Will you do if for me?'

'No problem', I thought, and I put the helmet on. We had just taken the second new ball and Colin Tunnicliffe was bowling. He immediately sent down a half-volley on the leg stump, and Glamorgan's Malcolm Nash whipped it off his toes and it smashed right through the grille and broke my cheekbone. What's more, the ball actually became wedged behind the bars, so I took it out and handed it to Eddie, who appealed for a catch.

Dickie Bird was one of the umpires and he didn't know what to do. After a lot of thought he called 'dead ball', and since then there has been a rule that if the ball hits a fielder's helmet, the batsman is not out.

Of course, the helmet gave me a false sense of security. If I hadn't been wearing one, I would have turned away once I saw the shot was being played.

Glamorgan batsmen must have disliked me, because my other bad knock on the head also came against the Welsh side when John Hopkins put me in hospital for two days. He swept Geoff Miller off the leg stick, and the ball struck me on the forehead and rebounded to slip, where he was caught.

Only the groundsman was free to take me to hospital, and I remember him making me comfortable on a bale of straw in the back of his car, and weaving through the streets of Cardiff and repeatedly sounding his horn. In the end I didn't know what was worse, the knock on the head or the hair-raising drive.

Though I fully understand the hazards of fielding close to the bat, I still don't like to see players wearing helmets in that position.

Helmets would never have come into cricket but for all the aggression that has followed on the greed for money. I think they are unnecessary. And I don't like the way some players keep passing them around deliberately to waste time.

If I could personally bring in a new rule I would insist that every batsman who goes to the wicket wearing a helmet should be made to wear it right through the session. Even against spinners.

I hate to see batsmen going backwards and forwards putting the helmet on and then taking it off. It's not fair to spectators. It ruins the flow of a game.

Brian Reynolds believes that bad pitches rather than faster bowlers are the main cause for batsmen seeking so much protection:

There are a lot of dodgy wickets around now. They have definitely deteriorated. Because of this I can understand a batsman wanting to try anything which will help him feel safe.

But the bowlers are no faster. And there can be nothing more ridiculous in a county match than experienced batsmen wearing helmets against harmless little spinners and medium-pacers. Yet if a helmet gives a batsman confidence, that is fine by me. What should be banned are helmets worn by close-in fielders.

Though I took several nasty knocks when I played, I'm certain I wouldn't have worn a helmet even if they were available.

David Gibson is one of many pace bowlers who have experienced the shock of hitting a batsman on the head and he now says:

Helmets are here to stay. There is so much short-pitched bowling now that I have no objection to batsmen putting them on. It's basic common sense.

The bouncer has become nasty. It no longer flies harmlessly over a batsman's head. The good bouncer is up under a batsman's throat now. And the Authorities were right to keep them down to one an over.

I twice hit a batsman on the head. Jim Parks was the first at Lord's. He didn't duck fast enough, but all I did was wake him up and he went on to score a hundred. Barrie Meyer was the other one. He's doing fine as an umpire now, so no damage was done there, either.

Even when close-in fielders wear helmets, they still rarely last more than two years in suicide positions, says Warwickshire's coach Alan Oakman, himself a brilliant close-to-the wicket catcher for England and Sussex in the fifties and sixties:

No matter how well a player is protected, he can only field in that position for a short time. His confidence will go. Sooner or later he becomes shell-shocked. He suffers so many knocks that in the end he is taking evasive action even before the ball is bowled.

I speak from experience. When I stopped fielding there, I was no longer leaning forward, looking for the ball. At the back of my mind I knew another knock could be seconds away. It was time for someone else to take over.

Every year I notice counties have new fielders standing close in. People crack. They take one blow too many. Wearing a helmet obviously provides extra protection for players in suicide positions, but their nerve still goes in the end.

Confidence is the key word. That's why so many batsmen are turning to the helmet. We didn't have them in my day because if we faced four fast bowlers in a season, we wondered where the other two had come from.

Bowlers are overdoing the aggressive stuff now. We were told to pitch the ball up. To beat the batsmen with swing. These days they aim at a batsman's ribs. It's a ploy: they hope the batsman will try to fend the ball off and give a catch to the man under the helmet, close in on the leg side.

Ray East emphasises that every Essex batsman wears a helmet whenever the occasion demands it, especially after seeing the luckless Alan Lilley struck several times in 1983. East says of Lilley, and helmets in general:

As he's such a gritty player, Alan didn't crack up. But because we now have helmets, I think a lot of quick bowlers believe they can't hurt batsmen any longer. So they thump the ball down, not thinking of the consequences.

Even at the nets I have had to speak to one seam bowler in particular because he keeps digging the ball in. I asked him once what he had in mind and he said 'But he has the helmet on. So I thought I'd let him have a few.'

Quick bowlers are deliberately pitching just short of a length these days. They place a fielder directly under a batsman's ribs and then slam the ball down, aiming it just below the heart. No batsman is spared this tactic. Even the number-eleven can expect a blast. I've taken more knocks around the ribs in the past two years than ever before.

I'm all in favour of the helmet. It can help a young batsman with the position of his head when facing a fast bowler. It gives him confidence. He stands firm, so his eyes are brought level.

The helmet certainly helped our young batsman Chris Gladwin. He was so confident in his first championship match that he went out and knocked up fifty. He played all his shots, just as he did when we first saw him as a sixteen-year-old schoolboy. Young batsmen often play in awe of big-name bowlers and go into their shell, but Chris didn't. He went out and played his normal game and was successful.

Just like their coaches, even the great West Indian batsmen can't fully agree on whether to wear a helmet or not.

On the one hand we hear from Lancashire's John Savage:

Whenever the subject of helmets comes up, I make the point that even Clive Lloyd will wear one if he thinks it is necessary. Every recognised batsman in this club has one. If it gives players confidence, I have no objection to them, though I don't think many batsmen would have worn them in my time.

I tried one in the nets once and couldn't play with it on. 'How the hell can they wear these things?' I kept asking myself.

Yet Peter Robinson says at Somerset:

With so many batsmen rushing off to put their helmets on I think it is interesting that you will never see Viv Richards wearing one. Helmets were not heard of when I played, so I'm not sure whether I would have worn one. Perhaps I might have been happier in one on certain pitches, particularly at Bath, which was notorious.

Stewart Storey comments:

Helmets are a new feature of the game, and though I approve of them being worn by batsmen I am strongly against them being used by fielders. I believe it comes under the heading of sharp practice. If a fielder is not brave enough to stand close in with only a box and shin-guards, he should not be there at all.

Wearing a helmet has become so badly abused in the field that some players are practically standing on a batsman's toes. They are exploiting the security a helmet provides.

If a helmet gives a batsman confidence I see nothing wrong

in his wearing one. There are more fast bowlers around now than any time before. The game has become much more dangerous.

The continued emphasis on speed bowling has left Kevin Lyons in no doubt that a batsman needs to protect himself with every piece of equipment available to him.

Lyons was present when Glamorgan's opening batsman Roger Davis was so nearly killed in Cardiff while fielding at short-leg. He recalls that incident with a grim warning of what can happen if players don't take advantage of the protective equipment now on the market:

Warwickshire's Neal Abberley put all his weight behind a ball from Malcolm Nash and it struck Roger a terrible blow on the head. He collapsed on the spot and all the players around him thought he was dead. Thank God he wasn't. But a helmet would have saved him altogether – I'm sure of that. Since then I haven't thought twice about whether players should wear headgear. I would have helmets at school, as well. You can't start too early.

Players have been struck on the head and never recovered. I had a very promising batsman at Cape Town University who was going right to the top. Then he was hit on the head and he never got into line again. For the lack of a helmet a brilliant career was lost.

Having said that, I still believe the bouncer is an essential part of the game and I would hate to see it outlawed.

Peter Sainsbury admits that he disapproved of helmets at first but then on seeing so many players hit on the head, changed his mind and now fully supports them.

Why be hit if you can avoid it? Helmets should be worn in matches, in the nets, at club level, and even by schoolboys.

We had a nasty situation when Bobby Parks was struck on the head at our indoor school. He was badly shaken and I was worried that he might lose his confidence. So I made him put on a helmet and I asked a couple of quick bowlers to slam a few short ones down at him. I wanted to see him sway and duck as the ball reared towards his head. Through working in the nets like that we achieved what we wanted. From then on he was rock-solid behind the ball, and he always wears a helmet against the quickies now.

It was important for him, and for us, that he didn't lose his nerve. Bobby is an outstanding wicketkeeper, indeed probably better than his father Jim, but he still needs to improve his batting.

I am always mindful of the damage, both physical and psychological, that a bad blow can do to a player. David Turner, our middle-order batsman, suffered badly in that respect. He was in great form during his best years and pushing hard for a Test place, when he tried to hook a slow long-hop from Tony Brown of Gloucester but misjudged the bounce and deflected the ball into his eye.

David was shattered. The injury set him back several years and all hopes of an England place were lost after that.

Nothing has changed more dramatically in cricket in the past ten years than the size and shape of the bats used by cricketers at all levels. Clearly the emphasis has been on manufacturing a piece of wood that will provide the maximum power, and for that reason they have become a great deal heavier and in some cases even too difficult to lift, especially for young schoolboys. The county coaches themselves are virtually unanimous in their positive dislike of heavy bats which, they say, destroy most attempts to play good quality strokes.

Opening the case for the opposition, Brian Reynolds says:
I see so many bats now that I would put on the fire. That's all they are good for. My bat weighed no more than 2lb 3oz, so I was surprised one day when I picked up Peter May's bat and found it as light as a feather. I asked him how much it weighed and he said it was all of 2lb 7oz. But the balance was perfect, and the pick-up absolutely beautiful.

Having the 'right' bat is often all in the mind, but it doesn't have to be heavy to be good. No two bats are the same, and I always made the point of selecting one that was heavy at the bottom because the balance is always very important when it comes to playing shots.

Keeping up this theme, Alan Oakman says:
In my day most players had bats that weighed between 2lb 3oz and 2lb 5oz. But now, because of all the limited-over

games, most players are preferring to use heavier bats. Brute force has taken over from elegance and style. Defensive shots have practically disappeared. And when did you last see a leg-glance? It can't be played with a heavy bat.

And where does England's graceful captain David Gower stand in the big-bat league. Does he, too, favour one of those prodigious clubs? His Leicestershire coach Ken Higgs says:

In no way. David has a nice, light bat. The heaviest bat I ever saw was the one Brian Davison used. I could barely pick it up.

The only time I played with a heavy bat I ended up in hospital. We were playing Notts at Trent Bridge and there were just four balls of our innings to go. Brian thought I needed to hit the ball into the Nottingham Forest football ground, so he made me borrow his bat. It was a terrible mistake because I got a nasty top-edge and the ball smashed into my mouth and I needed fifteen stitches. Worse than that, I was caught at mid-wicket! And when I came back from hospital the match was over – and we had lost.

I am sure many players turn to a heavy bat as an excuse. When they time the ball correctly, every bat is good. We've had several young players at Leicester who preferred a heavy bat, but the moment they failed to score runs they threw it away and pinched a light one from someone else.

Brian Davison was different. He was immensely strong – sheer brute force. I couldn't imagine Brian with a light bat. He'd break more than he could afford.

Graham Gooch is so fastidious about his bats that he has an inch and a half cut off the bottom of every one. With his upright stance he claims that this shorter bat provides the perfect pick-up and enables him to club the ball in baseball fashion.

Hampshire's improved all-rounder Mark Nicholas has the same Gooch-inspired stance and was so captivated by the amputated bat that he took one when Essex played at Southampton and laughingly refused to give it back.

Nicholas then used it for a month, but as it did little for his form he finally sent it back, adding the poignant postscript 'It's so damn short the ball keeps going underneath. For the first time in my life I'm being bowled by straight ones.'

Clive Lloyd wields a bat that weighs well over 3lb and his Lancashire coach John Savage admits, 'It's so heavy I can't pick it up. And it has seven rubbers on the handle to give him the right balance.'

Lloyd's exuberant West Indian colleague Eldine Baptiste is another batsman who has succeeded in having seven rubbers pulled onto the handle of his SS Jumbo. In fact I was at Lord's on the day before the Second Test in 1984 when Peter Edwards in the cricket shop had to concede defeat as the eighth rubber refused to go on.

Though chiefly a bowler in his playing days, David Gibson still enjoys watching batsmen at work and he says:

Heavy bats are destroying good players. Wicketkeepers and slip fielders rub their hands in anticipation when they see a batsman coming out with a large bat. Day after day batsmen go to play a shot, find they are not quite in the right position and then realise to their horror that the bat is too heavy to pull away. Snicks are inevitable with a heavy bat.

Peter Sainsbury agrees:

Roy Marshall was one of the strongest hitters we've ever had at Hampshire, but he didn't use one of those huge bits of wood I see so many people struggling with these days.

Doug Padgett is both bemused and outspoken on the subject of heavy bats and says:

I don't know how some chaps manage to lift them. I always used a light bat. About 2lb 3oz. Now they are 3lb and more. I don't see the point of so much wood. A ball can only go for four. A batsman doesn't score more if the ball goes faster over the ropes. And he doesn't get seven or eight if the ball lands in the tenth row of the Stand. It's a six, and that's the end of it.

By today's standards Geoff Boycott and Arnie Sidebottom are the only Yorkshire players using light bats. Boycott's is no more than 2lb 4oz. Personally I have no time for the very heavy bats. They feel uncomfortable in my hands and a bat must always feel right if a player is going to do well.

Basil d'Oliveira took the very first Duncan Fearnley bat to Australia and it worked so well, he scored 800 runs with it. Now d'Oliveira says:

Duncan still has it on display at his factory, and when I call there I always pick it up, though I can't believe I ever used it. The wood is so light. Hand me a bat like that now and I could never play with it. Over the years I have become very fond of my heavy bat.

At the start of every season a player will try out his equipment and for a day or two the whole lot will seem strange to him. It's the same with a heavy bat. You pick one up and you think 'I'll never get used to this.' But you go in the nets a few times, play one good innings, and you are married to it for life.

All players who field in the deep curse the heavy bat. As the ball skims across the ground they think 'I've got this one covered', only to find that the ball goes shooting past them. The heavy bat causes that. It makes fielders look fools.

Against these points, if a player likes to cut or hook, then a big bat must be a disadvantage. It is usually too heavy for him to pick up to execute those type of shots.

Sobers and Kanhai, and other great strokemakers, think we are mad for using such heavy bats. When they saw mine, which weighed about 2lb 7oz, they used to look at me in disgust.

Kanhai used to say, 'I see you've brought your tree again, Basil.'

Anyone who spends a whole six-month holiday facing a ferocious bowling machine that shoots out cricket balls at all speeds from sixty to 100 miles an hour might seem something of a masochist. Well, to Steve O'Shaughnessy such a spartan routine was all part of his dedicated plan to become established as a front-line county cricketer, with a special ability to cope with fast bowling.

Exuberant, keen, and a superb wind-up merchant, O'Shaughnessy made his Lancashire debut in 1980 and three years later hit the headlines by crashing 100 in just 35 minutes off the Leicestershire attack.

His obsession with the bowling machine, both at Old Trafford and on his visits to Lord's, prompted the wise-guys to crack that he's probably a sleeping partner in the company that manufactures them.

Yet to spend at least three days a week right through the winter diligently confronting the mechanical monster is a serious business, as chief coach John Savage knows better than anyone:

O'Shaughnessy has been clever. With so much short-pitched bowling these days, he knows the bouncer has become a terrific force in the game. A lot of people are lazy. They don't think about it. But not O'Shaughnessy. He's worked out a way to use the machine to his own advantage. He points it down at head height and faces tennis balls. He sets the speed at between sixty and eighty miles an hour and the balls come out like bullets. If he feels particularly sharp, he'll turn it up to a hundred.

In that case there's only a split second for him to duck or sway, but if he does get hit, then he's not hurt. It might sting a bit, but that's all. It's a smart way of learning how to tackle the bouncer, and it's paid off for him.

If you don't play a bouncer the bowler will soon get tired of slinging them down. It's when a batsman spars at them, and takes his eye off the ball, that he'll keep digging them in.

When Somerset bought their bowling machine it posed yet another novel challenge to the irrepressible Brian Close, and Peter Robinson recalls how eagerly Close took it on:

Close came up to me and said 'Right, let's see what this thing is like at eighty miles an hour'. And he played it well. Later on Tom Graveney faced it, but he struggled a bit. Their techniques were quite different. Tom was more graceful than Close, more on his toes.

Peter Roebuck faces our machine a lot now. It's usually set between fifty and sixty miles an hour for him, and he's used it to time his half-volleys and to restore his off-side play.

The machine is marvellous for working on a specific shot. The ball can be put on the same spot time and time again, and no bowler in the world can do that for a batsman.

Peter has always worked hard in the nets. He's usually here at nine o'clock on match days though the rest don't come in until 9.45. He has thirty minutes on the machine before anyone else is sighted. For a month leading up to the 1983 season he was at the nets at nine every morning. Just him, the machine and me.

Even as late as August he came to me and said he'd like a net two hours before going out to bat in a Sunday League match. He felt his on-side play was slipping back. He spent a good forty-five minutes facing the machine that day and then went out and scored fifty to help us win the match.

Ken McEwan, in particular, makes good use of the Essex machine at the Chelmsford Indoor School, though chief coach Ray East is deeply worried that someone somewhere is going to suffer a serious accident while facing one:

I have a very real fear that the bowling machine will kill someone in the end. Most counties have one now. A feeder, who is usually the coach, has to stand on a tall chair to put the balls in, and there is absolutely no protection for him.

It has to be dangerous when hitters like Ken McEwan and Graham Gooch are down at the other end. Just imagine what could happen if Gooch got hold of a half-volley and cracked it straight back. He hits the ball so hard, the feeder would never get out of the way in time. When Graham goes in to bat, the feeder takes his life into his own hands.

I remember Kenny having a nasty scare one day. He glanced a ball from the machine into the side netting and was actually stepping forward to pick it up when the feeder accidentally sent down another ball and it shot out at fifty miles an hour and struck Kenny on the toe. He was lucky it wasn't his head.

Leaving aside the dangers, I must say the machine has become a big asset, especially for a player who wants to polish up on a specific shot. Kenny came in one morning and wanted the machine set at sixty-five miles an hour, and for the ball to be pitched just short of a length and swinging away. He was getting ready to play in South Africa and said that this was the type of bowling he would have to face once he arrived. By using the machine we were able to place the ball on the same spot time and time again until Kenny was satisfied he was in good shape.

I must say no one has faced the machine at more than sixty-five miles an hour with us because we feel that that should be the maximum speed in the conditions that prevail at an indoor school.

Peter Sainsbury also believes in keeping the machine to a maximum, except in his case he does allow it to creep up to seventy, but only for the very best county batsmen:

The machine is a great modern-day help to coaches. Not many of us are able to teach a batsman how to play a bowler who is thumping the ball down at seventy miles an hour, or how to tackle someone with a booming outswing. So all we do is switch the machine on and it does the job superbly.

Don Bennett, however, doesn't entirely share this enthusiasm, and the Middlesex players themselves have cooled off. Bennett explains why they are using the machine less and less:

I think it has one serious disadvantage. Because the ball shoots out of a hole, the batsman has no time to move his feet into position to play his shot. Even against a bowler of Wes Hall's pace the batsman could see him approaching, pick up his rhythm and prepare for a shot. The machine doesn't give him this chance to be ready. He is left rooted to the spot, which is hardly good for his game.

At hard-up Derbyshire, coach Phil Russell longs for the day when some kind sponsor will ring up and say, 'You're missing out. I'm sending you a bowling machine.'

And do Leicestershire have a bowling machine?

'Yes – that's me,' says Ken Higgs. 'To be frank, I don't like them. If one was brought in here we'd never get the lads to bowl. They'd want to be batting all the time.'

Well, one man who will always remain grateful to the bowling machine is little Larry Gomes. For while Gomes piled up his runs with consummate ease in the 1984 Test series, his critics of old wondered what had caused this remarkable transformation, particularly in his backlift, which was now straight and positive.

Gomes revealed the secret after receiving his man-of-the-match award for his century in the Headingley Test. He said it was all due to the many hours he had spent alone practising against the bowling machine at Lord's.

He had decided on a new grip and had started to play straighter. As a result his technical fault – turning the bat to the leg side and playing across the line – had been rectified, and he had put himself back in favour after losing his place against Australia in the winter. 'I owe it all to hard work and the Lord's machine,' he said.

5

Discipline, training and the one-day game

A Broad smile crosses Brian Reynold's face when he recalls the night he put a curfew on his Northamptonshire players and England opener Colin Milburn came back late, lathered in sweat.

Northamptonshire faced an important match against Essex at Colchester next day and skipper Reynolds told every player that he would be on the hotel steps to make sure they were all back by 11.30 p.m.

Reynolds, now the county's firm, no-nonsense chief coach, recalls:

Everyone was back on time except Colin Milburn. So at 11.35 I went out into the street to look for him. I was a bit upset to say the least. Then I saw this large figure pounding towards me through the darkness. He ran up the steps and practically collapsed at the door. His face was bright red, and he was sweating so much it dripped off his chin and came through his shirt. He tried to speak, but he was huffing and puffing so much the words wouldn't come out.

I found a seat for him and he eventually cooled down and apologised. He had misjudged the distance between our hotel and where he had been dining with friends. Realising he was late, he had rushed all the way and reckoned he had shed something like three or four pounds. Rather than tick him off, I preferred to think the run had done him some good, so I left it at that.

Discipline is very important to me. No one will achieve anything without it. When I take a team away, I tell every player to be in bed by midnight. Six hours of concentrated effort on a cricket field under a scorching sun can drain even the fittest of us. I keep warning them that one night I shall visit their rooms and anyone not there will be in serious trouble. It is no idle threat. I mean every word.

The same applies to players who don't get to the ground on time. When that happens, I usually leave them out. I would rather travel with only ten players than include someone who couldn't turn up on time.

One morning I was at the ground by nine o'clock for a trip to Essex but when I boarded the coach I found we were a player short. He had overslept. I had to decide whether to play myself or literally go into the Northampton Town football ground next door and ask the lad painting the terraces if he fancied a game for us. He was on our books as an all-rounder, so I knew he had something to offer. The football club allowed him to play, and he scored forty in the first innings and kept us in the game.

The weather was extremely hot and over the three days I could see him gradually wilting. In the end, he had to come off.

Then on the way home he said to me, 'I used to think cricketers had an easy time. Now I know the truth.'

Players with dirty flannels, scruffy clothes and grubby equipment also stir me up. I want to know why they present themselves like that. And I tell them to clean up, or else. . . .

If a player looks the part, he has a chance of being the part. That's my motto.

Colin Page adopts the same hard line with his precocious fledglings in Kent. Tough, and sometimes even abrasive, Page won't tolerate bad manners, bad dress or bad behaviour.

A young second-team player was once reported to him for being rude to an elderly lady. Page was incensed. He called the player into his office and warned him of his future conduct.

Colin Page: We have a first-class reputation for good conduct. I am a stickler for neatness. If a lad dresses like a scruff, he'll play like a scruff. Sweat shirts and jeans are banned. We supply blazers to every player on the staff and we expect them to be worn with a matching collar and tie.

I am appalled when players from other counties arrive for a game without having shaved. They wouldn't go to an office like that. Yet a cricket ground is their place of work.

At Kent we deal very swiftly with bad apples. Before we sign a player we always try to find out how he conducts himself. He might be taking 150 wickets a season for his club, but that's not enough for us. He must know how to behave. And he must have the character to cope with the pressure of playing at county level.

Talented opener Neil Taylor is one player who could well thank Colin Page for the care and interest he took when youthful exuberance threatened to give the lad an inflated idea of his own importance.

Colin Page: Neil first came to me when he was ten, and I must admit there were times when I found him quite a handful. He was a very confident boy, even to the point of being cocky.

He needed to be disciplined. He needed to be pulled down a peg or two. That was my job. I have devised a few good ways of sorting people out who think they are God's gift to the game. To be fair, Neil did knuckle down and he is now proving to be a fine player with a big future.

Taylor did, however, step out of line in 1984 when he enjoyed a round of golf on the morning before a John Player game and was suspended for one match.

As a world-class cricketer Basil d'Oliveira thrived on his unquenchable enthusiasm to attack at all times. Now, as Worcestershire's genial chief coach, nothing has changed. He watches with sharp eyes and condemns with a sharp tongue:

For all our matches I sit on my own. Just me and my binoculars. Sometimes I roll up a newspaper and use it like a telescope. It's surprising how it focuses on one spot.

I want all my players to know where I sit. I want them to know that I watch every ball. That is important. To some extent, I suppose, I'm hard on them. I believe in discipline. And I say to them, 'If you behave like boys I will treat you as boys.'

Even in the evenings when we are away and they want a few beers, I say, 'Fine. Great. Do what you want to do. I'm not stopping you. But just remember you have a job to do in the morning.' If they drink too much or stay out late, I say nothing until next day. Then I do let rip.

I am not the easiest guy to get on with. I've been no angel in the game. But I can sit down and relax. I couldn't care a damn. I don't worry about what's going to happen next day. My motto is, don't do as I do, do as I say.

Of course they know who I am. They know what my career was like and how I played the game. After all, the stories do go around. So I say, 'All right, if you want to live that way, fine. But I'll make one stipulation. Provided you can show me out there that you can play, I won't bother you. But if you can't, then I'll have to take over.'

I think they accept that. If we hit a bad day I keep them back in the dressing-room for half an hour. I say, 'What do you think? What happened today? How do you feel about the game?'

It's an open debate. They can say what they wish. I always give them first say. Then I go back at them and say, 'This is what I saw.'

One day we were bowling just fourteen overs an hour and I was seething in my seat. Players were strolling around instead of getting on with the game. The session after tea on the second day is the worst period in cricket. The bowlers amble up and the batsmen keep pushing the ball back, just playing out time. Then next morning everyone wants to make a game of it. So at the end of the day I went in and said, 'Right, in no way are we going to bowl just fourteen overs an hour.' I gave them a roasting.

On another occasion I might blow my top over a silly shot. I remember one batsman in particular who was playing beautifully. He had scored well over thirty runs when the off-spinner came on and placed a man backward of square.

The first ball went down and the batsman picked it up and hit it in front of square and it went for four. I sat there watching, and I thought, 'You stupid b——.'

They had a mid-on and a mid-wicket. Then they stuck another man out there. The spinner tossed another one up and our batsman lifted the ball again, this time between two of those fielders.

I sat there boiling up. I knew what was coming. The next ball he whacked again, only this time the chap at mid-on ran to his right, threw himself forward and caught the ball.

When he got back to the dressing-room I said to our player 'That first shot you played, you knew they had a man there?'

He said 'Yes. I picked it up and I knew I could hit it in front of square.'

So I said, 'Oh, you are that good are you?'

'Yes. I knew I could hit it in front of square.'

So I said, 'What about the second one then?'

'I hit it between the two of them.'

I said, 'Fine. You are that good as well, are you? Well, don't give me that rubbish. I have played this game before and there is no way you can control a pick-up shot. A pick-up shot can go anywhere. There was a bloke down there. You shouldn't have taken him on. You should have cancelled him out. You should have said, "Right, they have another man there, I'm not interested in the shot." You finished on forty-six, but you could have scored a hundred today.'

So I asked him about his third shot. He said, 'Well, the bloke ran around and caught it.'

'Precisely,' I said.

'Three times you gambled. You could have been out on any of those shots.'

These are the things I must get across. It's guidance. Building an innings is a problem for most batsmen. They don't realise that they have four to five hours in which to play.

Sometimes I think, 'I'm tired of you lot. I'm going to play without a scoreboard.' The opposition might object, but I'd love to say, 'Look, you've got six hours in which to bat. There is no scoreboard, so just bat.'

A lot of batsmen also play across the line without realising it. With all the modern video equipment I can now show them what they are doing wrong. And many of them will say 'What! I didn't do that, did I?' They are stunned. They thought they were perfect.

When Kim Barnett took over as captain of Derbyshire, he was assured of Phil Russell's invaluable support, especially in seeing that the club's standard of discipline was maintained at the highest level.

Phil Russell: In particular I want to be sure all our players respect and adhere to the code of conduct laid down in our rulebook. Anyone who steps out of line is hit hard. We insist that blazers and ties are worn on the first day of every championship match, and for all Benson and Hedges games.

Jeans are not allowed for matches or practice. And if players don't obey the rules we penalise them. They are reprimanded. They soon know we are not messing about.

We try to employ reasonable people. All wild men are weeded out. If they don't fit in, they have to go.

Even if Glamorgan can't make much impression on the field these days, it doesn't mean they can't look the part before and after matches.

Kevin Lyons: Every Glamorgan player has been told to smarten up. Even a handbook has been produced to remind them of who they are, who they represent, and the need to project a good image.

Though no one is standing over them with a big stick, the club have said players will be punished if they don't do as they are told.

Personally, I can't stand players who are scruffy. There is no excuse for turning up like a tramp. It wouldn't be tolerated in any other profession.

Though Surrey regard their players as 'mature adults', the penalties are swift and severe should anyone step out of line.

David Gibson: Surrey players are expected to carry out their duties with the club at heart. Anything they do that brings themselves, the club or the game into disrepute will require some immediate disciplinary action. We have a set of rules which must be kept. If they are not, then the players are admonished in the same way as professional footballers. They are fined by the management. In exceptional circumstances the player might be suspended for one or two matches. And if what he does is extremely bad he could well be told to get on his bike.

If for some reason a player doesn't come back to the hotel until three in the morning and we have a poor result next day, and he was noticeably listless, strong words would be spoken.

The rules were made because people in the past didn't behave themselves.

We also like players to think they are going to the office, and to dress the part. Players are the game's shop window. They wouldn't go to work at the bank in T-shirts and jeans, so we don't let them come here dressed like that. Though, of course we don't expect them to travel in a car or coach in a three-piece suit.

Pat Pocock, our longest-serving player, sets a marvellous example. Pat's been here twenty years and he's always immaculately dressed. It's amazing how he comes up so fresh every season. He's never in a rut. He plays a lot of squash in winter and trains hard, which is probably the reason.

Of course, the older a player gets the more difficult it becomes for him to motivate himself. To work at his fitness. Pat's never been grease-lightning, but he's as fit now as he's ever been. And he's still one of the best off-spinners in the game. Everything he does is a credit to his self-discipline. He's a model for young players to follow.

Those who believe that only large men with loud voices can command respect on a cricket field will have reckoned without Keith Fletcher, diminutive and passive, but always firm and resolute when handing out the orders.
Ray East: If Fletch has a point to make, he really lays into you. Then an hour later we are all mates again. When it comes to dishing out the discipline no one escapes.

For all their tribulations Yorkshire, too, don't go soft on their troublesome players.
Doug Padgett: We treat the game seriously here. We expect people to dress properly. We expect them to be punctual. We come down hard on anyone seen walking about an hotel in jeans. Staying out late is not tolerated on any account. We won't have players wandering back in the early hours of the morning. If that happens they are taken to task. We throw the book at them.

We like players to use their heads when we go away. They are representing Yorkshire. We don't believe in having someone on duty in the hotel clocking them in, but we do expect them to behave like responsible adults. Treated in that way they are more likely to do their best for us. If I said, 'I want you all in bed by half-past-ten', three or four would probably rebel and nip down the fire-escape.

So we try to respect each other. And I think we get better results that way.

Meanwhile at Leicester it seems an inspired form of subtle cunning is being used to maximise effort and concentration.

Ken Higgs: Most of our players are on a one-year contract so they can't afford to be sloppy or lackadaisical. The committee decide who to keep and let go. Secretary Mike Turner does most of the hiring and firing, though he does seek my opinion.

It's a terrible job having to tell a player he's no longer wanted, but there's no room for sympathy in this game. One minute a player might be on top and the next he is out in the street. It happened to Roger Tolchard. He was our captain in 1983 but at the end of the season he was released. That's why cricket can be such a cruel game. That's why no one can afford to give less than 110 per cent.

Tolchard had to go to make room for Mike Garnham, a fine wicketkeeper who was born in Johannesburg but came to us from Gloucestershire.

I was here when he arrived. The only trouble was he thought he knew it all. I had to cool him down a bit. Plus the fact that I had ten other lads in my second team who knocked the stuffing out of him, which did him no harm at all.

Since then he has made good progress. He has come down to earth. He's realised that he still has a lot to learn. If he continues to improve at his present rate I see no reason why he shouldn't play Test cricket.

He did a great job for us in 1983. He led both our second team and our Under-25 side to championship successes. The lads respected him for what he did and I think they did him a big favour. He is definitely a lot more mature now.

Garnham, however, slipped back into bad habits twice in a month in 1984 when he was fined, and suspended for two matches for verbal abuse on the field.

Meanwhile at Edgbaston the lanky Alan Oakman is particularly anxious about life's temptations, and the way a lad can be led astray if not properly supervised:

When young players live alone or in digs, they tend to get bored, so we are looking for a hostel to accommodate them. A place where a woman can go in and cook their meals and look after their laundry.

Fit, athletic lads will always be a worry. They may get

muddled up with a girl, stay out late or wear ear-rings. It's all part of growing up. With a little luck and good club discipline they usually sort themselves out and in five years are established in the team.

Most players go through it. Trouble is not all of them remember it. Some of them, of course, don't wish to. I've had young players turning up with no spikes in their boots. Or no bootlaces. Even no boots. Then someone will forget his bag. Or he won't be wearing a vest. We are always telling them to wear a vest – it soaks up the sweat. Then we have those who wander around the field. Dreamers who forget to back-up at the bowler's end. One player left all his equipment behind after a game and didn't think about it until we were fifty miles up the motorway.

Cars are the curse of my life. Dozy players are forever coming in and saying they've slammed the doors and left the keys inside. One player had a puncture on the way to a match and when he opened the boot he didn't have a spare.

Whenever we drive past factories, I always say to our lads, 'Count yourselves lucky, you could be in there.'

With few exceptions county coaches are reluctant to enthuse too strongly about a player's ability or conduct, believing, I suppose, that such extravagant praise could lead to swollen heads and lazy performances.

So, taking all that into account, John Savage's observations on young bowler Mike Watkinson must be seen as something special:

If I were asked to name one young professional cricketer who could set an example for smartness, temperament and good behaviour, it would be Mike Watkinson every time. He is always immaculately dressed and absolutely dedicated to the game.

He's also done one hell of a job with very little experience. He played more first-class cricket than second-team matches in his first season, which was quite amazing.

The discipline here is as strict as anywhere. We never go soft on players. We are particularly fussy about our image and insist that every player wears his club blazer and tie on the first evening of every match.

Gloucestershire's Graham Wiltshire says emphatically:
Good discipline is an obsession with me. I will not tolerate bad behaviour, though the best type of discipline has now gone from the game.

I preach to our lads that if they are caught at the wicket, nicking, they must walk. In Gloucester we were brought up on a diet of George Emmett and Jack Crapp. Two wonderfully honourable men. With them you had to walk. No sulks. No hanging around. They would have cut off your head.

Fighting words, but echoed with equal ferocity by Ken Taylor:
I look for effort and contribution. Players are rewarded here for the work they do. I have no time for scroungers or cheats.

I don't mind how they dress for practice, but when we go away I insist they wear something connected with Nottinghamshire Cricket Club. On special occasions we wear blazers and ties. We tog up. At Buckingham Palace we all wore green blazers and everyone was impressed. If we wore them all the time there would be no special occasion, and they would get shabby. Jeans and T-shirts are definitely out. We must present the best image. If someone is a slob he has no right to a good living.

If anything in particular has helped to destroy the good old discipline that once existed in clubs I suppose it must be the frantic, country-wide scampering to all the one-day matches. In many cases players no longer have the chance even to shower after a day in the field before they are racing up the motorway to the next limited-over game. There's barely time to fix a knot in the mandatory tie.

Yet for all this hustle and bustle, Somerset's Peter Robinson, chief coach to the one-day experts, defends the new game with all the zest and purpose he once displayed as an opening batsman:
We can all sit back and grumble that the one-day game is spoiling this or that, but the plain truth is, it has kept me in a job. And I'm not the only one. A lot of mediocre players would have left first-class cricket a long time ago but for the one-day game. It has enabled the medium-pacer who can bat a bit, to remain on the staff a little longer. Hammering a few runs on a Sunday, and bowling eight overs for a few runs has kept him alive.

Our Keith Jennings is a good example. He's a one-day player. He's taken very few wickets in three-day matches. He would have struggled to stay on the staff without the one-day game. In all his years of first-class cricket he's taken only 96 wickets and virtually all of them have come in one-day matches. Someone like Keith is an average player, but the one-day game can turn people like him into overnight heroes.

I don't believe one-day cricket has ruined the quality of any English batsman as some people seem to think. Viv Richards has played as many one-day games as anyone else and you can hardly say it's affected his Test match performances. The top players are still good one-day cricketers.

Unlike Robinson, you get no loud applause from Doug Padgett when discussing the merits of the one-day game:

In my day we said it took three years of playing in a county side for someone to know what was going on. That was his apprenticeship.

In those times we played twenty-eight first-class matches, possibly more, because we played sides like the MCC, Cambridge University, Oxford University, and whatever country happened to be on tour. At Yorkshire we probably played thirty-one first-class games. Now we are down to twenty-one. So if it took three years for a player to reach his peak then, how long does it take him now?

On top of that the player today has all the different one-day games to work out. He has to improvise so much. That's probably why we are seeing such poor bowling actions and more batsmen hitting across the line. One-day cricket has caused this drop in standards. It's destroyed quality. It's a game for sloggers now.

It puts pressure on all county coaches like me. We are constantly being told that we no longer produce Test-match players. I agree. But don't blame the coaches. Blame all this one-day cricket that's wrecking our game.

If players don't adapt to one-day cricket they are out on their necks. All of a sudden counties are crying out for people who can thump the ball, play across the line, lift their heads and slog. We never played cricket that way. The forty-over game is the real menace. Clubs actually prefer to be 210 for nine than 170 for 1. And bowlers are instructed to contain and defend – not to bowl people out. That's depressing.

When I start to coach a youngster, he must have some ability. No one can take a lad out of a school side and say, 'Right, I'm going to make you a first-class cricketer.' If he has talent, I try to bring it out of him. I concentrate on basics. I try to make him a good orthodox player. This is important because once he's mastered the basics he is able to improvise. He's the lad who comes through.

Perhaps the most objective view on our one-day cricket comes from someone like Kevin Lyons, who has spent the past ten winters coaching in South Africa:

Compared with South Africa far too much one-day cricket is being played over here. As a coach I believe we could do without the Sunday League for a start. Prize money for this competition was as big as the three-day championship until a sponsor came forward in 1984. The championship had been overshadowed and devalued. Now that Britannic Assurance have put up £50,000, the championship should become more of a competition for players and spectators alike.

Having to adjust from one-day cricket to a three-day match is often too much for a young player. Limited-over games are doing enormous psychological damage. Championship matches should be played over four days, and more spinners should be brought into the game.

Peter Sainsbury agrees with Lyons and then goes further in suggesting that the one-day game must be the root cause of England's dismal decline in Test match standards.

Peter Sainsbury: When the John Player matches started I remember being invited to a committee meeting to discuss the best ways of approaching this forty-over game. And I remember the chairman turning to me and saying 'You're not certain of getting in, of course.' I said nothing, but I vowed under my breath that I would never miss a game. He was obviously stirring me up. Just what a good captain would do. So for those Sunday matches I varied my game. I became a different type of bowler. I adjusted my style. I bowled quicker and flatter and I played in every game.

If players don't impress in one-day matches they are often

dropped and forgotten about overnight. I wouldn't mind a pound-note for every good player who has been lost to international cricket in this way.

Taking his usual philosophical look, Basil d'Oliveira throws up his arms and says:

When I am coaching in the nets and I see a lad whacking the ball over the top I think 'What a dreadful shot'. So I tell him about it. And he stands there with his hands on his hips, all smug, and says 'What happens if I have to bat on a Sunday? If I don't practise those shots, how will I ever play them in a match?' There's no answer to that. I feel sorry for young players today.

Given the opportunity, Colin Page says he would happily use his pruning scissors on a fixture list that has 'got completely out of hand'. The introduction of so many one-day matches has made it impossible for players to perform at a consistently high level. He says:

Many times I have seen physically-exhausted players virtually praying for rain to get a break. When people like Graham Dilley are asked to bowl flat out for seven days a week there comes a time when they can give no more.

Can you imagine a professional footballer agreeing to travel three hundred miles to bowl thirty overs in six hours under a blazing sun? And what about the fielding? Every ball has to be chased, picked up and thrown in. The concentration is terrific. The players come in absolutely drained. Then all they can do is have a quick shower, jump in their cars and drive two hundred miles for a Sunday match.

There is no disputing that those opposed to the one-day game, especially the John Player League, are many and vociferous. Along with Somerset, it seems that Warwickshire are the only other county who categorically come out in favour of the competition. Alan Oakman states their case:

With so much limited-over cricket it was difficult for anyone to settle on a balanced side, so when Bob Willis took over as captain we realised we didn't have the strength to win three-day matches so we concentrated more on the one-day game.

To Warwickshire's credit, they won the John Player League in 1980, reached a NatWest final in 1982 and a Benson and Hedges final in 1984. Northamptonshire have also sampled the fruits of one-day success so it's not surprising that Brian Reynolds goes a long way to supporting Warwickshire's attitude and sticks his neck out when he says:

I am not one of the crowd who keeps saying we must have three-day cricket to produce first-class players. Having said that, I have no great love for the forty-over game which is nothing more than a glorified slog and makes it increasingly difficult for the older players to compete.

More disparaging stick for the John Player League comes from Ken Taylor and Don Bennett, who make no attempt to conceal their feelings. Taylor:

I also watch football and it's getting quite frantic. Young people seem to enjoy it, but I find it rather boring. In the same way people want to see all this crash-bang-wallop cricket. They want the one-day entertainment. Our membership is around four thousand and most of the older ones still prefer to watch the three-day game. I go along with that. There is no substitute for quality.

Don Bennett: The 55 and 60-over games are good, competitive events for players and spectators. The 40-over match is more of a sprint and played in front of a different type of spectator.

I would like to see the three-day championship matches continue, but reduced to sixteen in the season. And I would prefer it if no championship games were played on the same days as Test matches. In that way counties wouldn't suffer when their best players are away with England.

Lancashire offer trials to about fifty quick bowlers every winter but very few come through. John Savage is convinced that it's all due to the various Leagues playing limited-over matches. Explaining his theory, he says:

All games in the Lancashire League are now limited to 34 overs a side. When I played up there, the first side batted at two o'clock, declared at 4.40, and the other side went in.

Now, if the professional in a League side happens to be a bowler, he is going to send down seventeen of those overs.

That leaves just seventeen to be shared by the others. So if a young spinner comes on and bowls two bad balls in two overs he's immediately taken off. That's why the spinner has disappeared from first-class cricket. He no longer has a chance to do his apprenticeship.

The John Player League is just as bad. Quick bowlers amble in off ten to fifteen yards, drop the ball on the same spot for five or six overs, bat at number seven or eight, and that's enough. That's why we are being swamped by medium-pacers.

Though the limited-over game, and the John Player League in particular, take a battering from the coaches in general, David Gibson does make the point that these competitions have forced players to reach a standard in fielding and tactics that the old-timers would never have thought possible. He admits:

When I played the pattern never changed. In fact, I don't think we could have switched straight from a three-day match to a one-day game. Players have to be more versatile now.

Tactics are more important now than ever before. When Surrey are about to face someone like Viv Richards we always meet and pool our ideas on the best way to curb him – if there is one. In Viv's case we aim to frustrate him. To restrict his shots. Bowlers are told to attack his off stump and be sure not to drop them short. If they stray down the leg side he'll murder them. Everyone knows Viv is not the world's best starter. He likes to ease his way into an innings. So we work hard not to give him anything loose in his first five overs. Bowl well at Viv early on and he usually gets keyed up. That's when he's vulnerable. That's when he's likely to take a risk and have a whack.

Bowling to Ian Botham is quite different. We tell our players to pitch the ball just short of a length on the off stump. We stick to the motto – never give a good batsman room to play his shots.

Another important effect of one-day cricket is that players now need to be at their peak from the very first ball of the season. No longer is there time to warm up. They go straight into important tournaments like the Benson and Hedges, NatWest and the Sunday League. So it's imperative that they are physically and mentally ready.

Stewart Storey: Fitness has become a major requirement. Speed and agility are vitally important now. I go along with what Freddie Trueman and Alec Bedser used to do. They bowled themselves back into shape. When they returned after a winter lay-off they were usually carrying a stone overweight. So they bowled and bowled. They worked hard to trim down to get their breathing right.

At Sussex we've been trying to get ourselves fitter year by year, but each time we've ended up with more annoying injuries. Particularly with backs and groins.

I've come to the conclusion that players can be overtrained. Our outdoor nets usually start in April when the weather is still quite chilly. Bowlers build up steam and they sweat, and then they hang around while they cool off. This can only end in cramped muscles and chills.

And we've made the same mistake on match days. Players have loosened up by running around the ground and going through a series of warm-up exercises. Then they've gone back to the dressing-room and sat there for forty minutes and stiffened up. The sweat has dried off and the muscles contracted. We've gone looking for trouble.

We are putting more emphasis on the practicalities of the game now. We are paying more attention to batting, bowling and fielding.

Imran is a bit of an exception. He usually finds a quiet corner before matches and concentrates on a set of exercises which he thinks suit him best. He knows that his strength comes from the suppleness of his back. He is a fitness fanatic. Basically he is left to himself whenever possible, though I have to be careful not to let him have too much leeway and upset the other players. On no account must I create a feeling that there is one rule for Imran and another for the rest.

I'm forever walking a tightrope. I work on hunches and gut feelings. On how people seem to be. I have to judge how long I can remain optimistic and say pleasant things, and when I'm going to let fly and say, 'That was a bloody dreadful performance.'

I prefer to deal man-to-man. You can't rouse a cricket team in the way you wind up rugby players.

Meanwhile, up in Derbyshire, Phil Russell had just finished one of his special fitness sessions. His shattered players had flopped down on the dressing-room bench, spreadeagled their legs and thanked God it was all over . . . until the next day.

As Derbyshire's chief coach he's the best sergeant-major in cricket. Only in his case the traditional raucous bark is noticeably missing. Instead, all his urgent demands are made in a soft, almost persuasive tongue that belies the strength of a man who knows what he wants, and usually gets.

One of his batsmen, Kevin Brooks, was looking so ill after a fortnight's training that Russell had become intensely worried:

The lad had lost so much weight I thought he had cancer. I was terrified. I told him he had to eat. That he couldn't get fit without eating. He was desperately weak and drawn, and said he had stopped eating breakfast and cut back drastically on his other meals.

He had a diet, but the diet was for a businessman who sat at his desk all day, not for someone who was doing fifteen-yard shuttles, running three miles around a racecourse, followed by ninety minutes of bowling in the nets, and having to do his fielding practice as well. Only a small number of calories were allowed on his diet, and he probably burnt them up in just one shuttle. No wonder he looked like death. So I made him eat egg and toast in the morning, and have sandwiches for lunch. Then he started to pick up.

It was Eddie Barlow who started this fitness idea. We were bottom of the championship table and Eddie was captain. He said we needed a common denominator to bring the side together because, although we were a happy club, we weren't playing with a lot of spirit.

We lacked aggression and determination on the field. Basically it was a psychological problem. We trained hard under Eddie and did a lot better the following season. We were all very fit and it gave us a mental approach that we hadn't experienced before.

I think we've maintained that level ever since, though in some cases, like Kevin Brooks, players have gone too far and lost too much weight. They've forgotten that cricket is very much a stamina game. Fred Swarbrook suffered in his first season. He was a bit overweight, trained hard and thought, because he got fit, he was halfway to taking wickets – but a player must still practise his skills. It affected Fred psychologically and in the end he literally couldn't bowl. He came to a complete stop.

To make sure our players stay fit through the winter, I set each one of them specific targets, depending on their ability as athletes, of course. For some it might be a three-mile run while for others it might be sprints or press-ups. And that's what I ask them to do when they come back in April. Perhaps it will be fourteen shuttle-runs in four minutes, or twenty sit-ups. And I expect them to come back fit and be able to do what I ask of them.

In the first week we do a lot of running so that I can test them. Then we concentrate on skills. If they are not fit, then they are not capable of working on their skills. That's how I see it. Of course some players have to work harder than others, especially those who only have to look at a potato and they put on a pound.

Enhancing his reputation as a raconteur, Ray East tells a lovely story of the time England bowler Neil Foster joined the Essex staff and disheartened the older members with his youthful exuberance. Holding back the chuckles, East says:

When 'Foss' came to the ground we were lining up for our first pre-season run and some of the slower pros went up to him and literally begged him to take it easy. Not to go charging off and show them up.

But Foss couldn't resist the challenge. For the first mile of our three-mile slog he stayed well behind with the pack. Then all of a sudden he burst away and raced fifty yards ahead of everyone else. Eventually we all got back to where we started and he received a few hard glares and more 'kind' words of advice.

But Foss couldn't control himself. Next day he went tearing off again and we could just pick him out in the distance when we noticed him coming to a stop. Then he started to hobble a bit. When we caught up with him we found that he had pulled a muscle and was in a lot of pain, though he didn't get much sympathy from the rest of us.

In fact, we all had a good laugh at him, though the joke

soon rebounded on everyone. About three days later we again staggered in, knackered, on our knees after another three-mile run, and found Foss lying on his back, his hands behind his head, relaxing on the physio's bench with the physio running the treatment lamp up and down his leg.

David Acfield was far from pleased. I remember him falling through the door and grunting 'Just look at him. Don't some people learn fast!' David is the meanest bowler in the game. He literally counts every run that's taken off him. He's even gone and corrected the scorers.

Pre-season training is extremely hard at Essex. We do a lot to build up stamina. Besides all those three-mile runs, we jog, sprint up and down hills and do all kinds of stretching and loosening-up exercises. John Lever is our sergeant-major. You obey his orders or suffer the consequences. Not many people disobey.

We do our roadwork in the mornings and go to the nets after lunch. The roadwork is so hard that I got back one day and didn't have the breath to speak. I just slumped in a chair, shattered.

Keith Pont cheered us up after one slog when he joked that if anyone could hit a ball three miles, an Essex player would be the first to get it back.

Basil d'Oliveira is far from impressed by those counties who spend week after week working on complicated fitness routines and running the soles off their shoes:

I have firm views on physical fitness. I believe every county cricketer should get himself fit without having to run around a park a hundred times every day for a fortnight. His fitness routine should always include a bat and a ball. We return in the first week of April, and our training programme includes just thirty minutes to loosen up and then it's straight into the nets. If a player has any pride in himself he should come back in good shape.

To help our bowlers I cut a strip the width of three stumps and tell them to keep pitching the ball on a length in that area.

Players should be told to spend more time with bat and ball and be given less of this mountain climbing. Fielding is also important. Far more important than trotting round the park.

To polish up their fielding, Surrey drastically altered their pre-season training in 1984 and for the first time called in a physical fitness expert to take the players through a series of exercises with the accent on speed and stamina.

David Gibson: He gave the players a tough session every morning for three weeks. A bit different from my time, when all we did was jog a few laps around the ground and finish off with some knees bend, arms stretch. Then everyone went in the nets and batted and bowled all day.

There is much more emphasis on fitness now. It helps players to think clearly. It puts their mental attitude right. Sharpens them up. And it's definitely helped with the overall standard of fielding. In my day if we got green on our flannels we had usually tripped over.

In the past years there's been a marked shift away from net practice. It can get boring and counter productive. We prefer to play practice matches out in the middle, and to concentrate more on our fielding.

I can remember when John Edrich started. He found it terribly hard to throw a cricket ball. But he worked at it and, though he never became a rocket thrower, his length and accuracy did improve with practice.

Opener Graham Barlow supervises all the pre-season training at Middlesex and this, too, spills over into polishing up on the fielding skills.

Don Bennett: I have long lost count of the players Graham has taught by sheer example. I have often seen him knocking the stumps down with a throw from way out in the covers.

I must admit we've been lucky to have Barlow and Roland Butcher in the same side. Both of them practise extremely hard. They spend hour after hour just picking the ball up at great speed and then throwing down the stumps. When youngsters see it done that way, they have to be impressed. So in the end we have everyone doing it.

Schools don't pay enough attention to fielding, but it's a vital part of the game. It's a skill. What good is a batsman if he averages thirty and then drops at least one catch and gives away forty in the field?

In the past few years we've stepped up on our pre-season

work. We get rid of the rust in the gym for a week, which includes a lot of abdominal exercises, and then we switch to sprints and four-mile runs. But we don't overdo the running. Some counties do a lot more than Middlesex. I feel we are preparing for a cricket season, not the Olympic Games.

In keeping with other counties, Lancashire think hard about their pre-season training and settled for one of the most original preparations in 1984 when they flew to Spain to take advantage of the sun in La Manga.

John Savage, tanned and cheerful, said:

Fifteen of us went out for eight days at the end of March. We played a few matches on a beautiful pitch and then came back and went straight up to an hotel in the Lake District for a week. We trained in the mornings and played golf in the afternoons. It was a good way to relax before the pressures of a hard season.

Enthusiasm to practise during the winter was so strong among Lancashire's younger players that Savage became worried that rather than sharpen their game, the lads could become stale and jaded:

Players like O'Shaughnessy, Allott, Fairbrother and Folley all virtually demanded that they should come in several times a week from November to April. It was great to see them so keen, but I did worry that one or two might get stale as the season went on.

I think too much cricket is being played now. Some lads might be better off with a complete break, and not just thumping golf balls. Once a season is over they should take a rest and forget the game for a month or two and then come back fresh.

Obviously some players can cope with pressure better than others. Clive Lloyd is the perfect example. He's played twelve months of the year for as long as I can remember. And he nets and trains, as well. He baffles me. To be honest, I have no idea how he does it. Of course the constant playing has taken its toll. His knees are no longer what they used to be. But he doesn't moan. And you'll never catch him dodging matches. Clive has worn spectacles all his playing life, but his eyesight has never troubled him. He tried contact-lenses once, but they didn't seem to work.

I always preach to my players that a cricketer can have all the ability in the world, all the coaching, but he'll never achieve anything unless he is dedicated. He must practise, talk, and think the game. Then, if he has ability, he may just make it.

All Lancashire's practice and purpose paid off handsomely in 1984 when they captured the Benson and Hedges trophy, totally overwhelming Warwickshire in the final at Lord's.

Yorkshire begin their pre-season training on the first Monday in April. Players loosen up with a few runs and physical exercises in the mornings, and then move on to the nets after lunch.

Doug Padgett: This routine continues for four weeks, and then towards the end of April we introduce a few practice matches. We mix them up. We have a two-day game, a 55-over game, and then we play representative sides from the Yorkshire League, Bradford League and Huddersfield League.

We believe matches of this sort give us the best preparation. We started on this idea after dropping fixtures with Oxford and Cambridge. The professionals in the Leagues give us more of a test.

Down in Wales, Kevin Lyons admits that some Glamorgan players didn't take kindly to the training led by Alan Jones and Mike Selvey in the spring of 1984:

Alan and Mike worked out a stiff programme to get the lads fit. When the weather was good they put them in the nets, but every morning was devoted entirely to physical exercises and long runs, which never proved popular.

One day Mike sent them on a six-mile slog along the riverbank and they came back dragging their feet, and moaning and groaning. Players shouldn't need to grumble like that. They shouldn't be out of puff. They should be fit. Trouble is some don't do enough in winter to keep themselves in condition. That's where a lot of the fault lies.

6

Temperament and technique

Don't be deceived by David Gower's calm, unruffled composure at the batting crease. For behind that pale, passive exterior is a heart that beats hard with every ball bowled at him.

No one knows Gower's innermost cricket feelings better than his Leicestershire coach Ken Higgs, and this former England bowler is quick to dismiss as a myth the talk that Gower is totally nerveless and without a care in the world:

A lot of people make out that David doesn't worry. Well, that is not true. David is a constant worrier.

He takes his cricket seriously. Even in a benefit match he is determined to get runs. He is a perfectionist. He likes to prepare himself properly for a match or a long tour abroad. And not just physically, but mentally as well.

Before he toured the West Indies, I remember him grabbing our young bowler Gordon Parsons at the indoor nets. He asked him to stand halfway down the wicket and to throw cricket balls at him and to make them bounce. Then, as they flew at his head, David stepped inside the line and hooked them sweetly. And that was only to get himself mentally ready for the bouncers the West Indians bowl these days. To get himself in tune for Marshall, Holding and the others.

That's the type of work the public never see. They rarely know how much is done behind the scenes.

Though a strong believer in coaching and practice, Ken Taylor takes great care to emphasise the need to be cautious and, in particular, to think twice before altering a player's stance or technique. The thoughtful Nottinghamshire manager says:

When players reach a particular standard, all a coach should do is try to improve them, not to change them. Overdoing the job can be the biggest danger of all. I was twenty-eight when a certain coach tried to alter me completely and I got in a frightful tangle.

Take the case of Derek Randall. If a coach was trying to make a name for himself and got hold of Derek, he would finish him off for good.

Derek is just a natural. I was chairman of our cricket committee and Brian Bolus was captain when I said, 'Let's give this lad a go. Let's see what he can do.'

Derek was about twenty at the time and he went in and scored eighty, hitting sixes and fours all over the ground. He came to us from the local league, in which we now run a side – deliberately to find out how players react to the game. It's strange, but once they come down to the county, many of them fold up. The occasion is too big for them.

Derek Randall is a good entertainer. An amusing bloke. But he doesn't arrive at anything logically. He gets confused. He has no way of working back on how he is doing things. He is a clown, really – like Norman Wisdom. I remember him reversing his car into a lamp-post and he stood behind it, holding up the bumper, just like Norman Wisdom would have done. He's always hitting things with his car. And sometimes, when he is bowled out, he looks as though he can't understand why fate has been so unkind. He can't believe it has happened to him.

He's not a wit or a joker – he's just a clown. He wouldn't need to be trained. And he worries like hell. It's just as well his wife is cool. She keeps him intact.

I remember we played Surrey at the Oval and everyone, including the umpires, had told us not to pad up to Sylvester Clarke. We hadn't played much against him, so we didn't know his strengths. After one of our openers was out, Derek went in and was out first ball, padding up to Sylvester.

Then we went up to Harrogate and Derek did the same thing again, and he was lbw for the second time. So I called him in and told him what he was doing was ridiculous. I said it obviously followed that it was not right.

And he looked at me and said, 'Well, no, it's not like that. It's an improvement.'

I said, 'How can that be an improvement?'

'Well, last year I would have been caught in the slips!'

I could see no logic in that. It didn't make sense.

And he gets very het up. He gets quite bothered at times. He listens to the wrong people. To be honest, he's not sure who he should be listening to. The snag is he is not someone with a strong character and, as he can't always work things out for himself, he has to listen to someone.

We certainly didn't change his stance or technique. He changed all that when he played for England. They told him straightaway. They said he was wrong, so they changed him completely.

Oh yes, he used to fidget about, but he always stood up. He always played straight. All the best batsmen play standing up. Once you bend or stretch, your cricket is going wrong. I suppose he still gets away with it, but that's because he has such enormous ability.

Coming from North London, I played against Denis Compton when he was fifteen. When I first saw Derek, I thought he was the most natural player I had seen since Denis. But Denis was protected by Patsy Hendren. He wouldn't let anyone interfere with the way he played. And he was a strong character, anyway. He calmly went on and didn't worry.

How Derek can score 170 in that Centenary Test and then be told he has to change makes no sense to me at all. If you watch a film of that innings you will see that Derek had a very different stance from what he has now. I feel very strongly about it. What they did was obviously wrong.

Without being biased, they leave me baffled. Derek came back from the 1982 Australian tour top of the averages, but when the summer came round they left him out and picked Mike Gatting. And Gatting didn't even go on tour. Even worse, they took Derek away from us and made him twelfth man in all the World Cup games.

I don't understand their thinking. Derek himself is completely illogical, so perhaps *he* knows what they are up to. But he must have wondered what he was doing, just sitting there, when he had topped the averages.

Derek wasn't the only one to suffer. The same happened to Brian Bolus. Once he was picked for England, he became a new chap. He used to come in and whack the new ball. He was a most exciting player to watch. He had bags of guts. But once he played for England he hardly hit the ball in anger again. Brian was a strong character, so how they ever changed him I shall never understand. If these players are good enough to get in the side, why the hell change them?

To be frank, I don't agree with the set-up at all. England should have a full-time manager. He would build the side, and the people he picked would play as he wanted them to. And continue to play that way. He would make sure he chose the right people or he would be out of a job.

I've had a lot of experience of committees, and I'm not being offensive about anyone who might serve on one when I say I can't understand how they can ever run anything. They nearly always arrive at a compromise. There is no way of acquiring any consistency, plan, or the feeling of being together as one. A compromise is the first step to failure.

Micky Stewart would be my choice as England manager. He has played Test cricket and has had experience outside the game, which I think is important. He would need three years to sort things out. He would carry the can. Who carried the can for the England shambles in New Zealand and Pakistan? And the behaviour of some players?

Taylor points out that Basharat Hassan is another Nottingham player no coach could help, and admits:

I don't understand his batting at all. He must have the most peculiar stance in cricket, but he still does the basic thing right – he gets behind the ball. He is always in line. I've watched him time and time again, but I can't think of anything else that he does correctly.

'Bash' is a gutsy chap. A good player when the pressure is on. I remember we were 20 for 4 against Surrey and Sylvester Clarke had taken a hat-trick, but 'Bash' weathered the storm, scored 91 not out and we won the match off the last ball. It's strange, but he's never been happy about batting as an opener, yet he plays the quickies as well as anyone, and hooks them all. I remember in our championship year we ran into trouble against Sussex, but he took on Imran and Le Roux and scored 80 to give us a chance.

By now I've lost count of the times he's been hit on the head and in the face. He's terribly unlucky that way. All his teeth were knocked out in one game, so I finally persuaded him to wear a helmet.

He shows the same courage at short-leg. Nothing puts him off. You can hit him all day and he'll still stand there. He's going to be hard to replace in that position.

Right through his career as an England opener, Chris Tavare's unusual batting grip provoked comment and despair from the purists who believed he was practically eliminating any chance of playing a good, natural attacking shot. His Kent coach Colin Page is one of those who disapproved, and is frank and severe in his criticism. Tavare was a mere ten-year-old when Page first admired the boy's talents at the Sevenoaks Indoor School:

If Chris had a fault as a lad, it was his flippancy. He wouldn't knuckle down. At twelve and thirteen it was hard work trying to get him to take batting seriously.

His unusual grip is often brought up as a topic of conversation. All I know is that during his teens he had the textbook grip, and he was extremely successful with it. Everything seemed to change when he went to play for England. That's when this new grip came in. For some reason he seemed to think it made him better equipped for the world's fastest bowlers. And at least one senior player in the England team had a big influence on the change.

Chris is a fine stroke-maker, and there are times when I am sure this grip is not doing his play justice. He is a thoroughbred. And one of his big assets now, and so different from his early days, is his serious and thoughtful attitude to the game.

At some time in the season it's inevitable that even the very best players find their form slipping slightly and when that happens at Kent they usually go back to Page for a pep talk and reassurance:

When they come to me in those circumstances I treat them all as gentlemen. And nearly always their trouble is loss of confidence. It's when they start to feel sorry for themselves that I read the riot act. I don't go soft on anyone, no matter how many England caps they might have. Like good captains, good coaches must know how to handle people. They have to be good psychologists, as well.

There seems little doubt that if a national survey were taken to find the player who took his cricket most seriously, Dennis Amiss would figure very close to the top.

Warwickshire coach, Alan Oakman, is full of admiration for Amiss's dedication and says of him:

He is the most self-critical player I have ever known. I have seen Dennis come back to the dressing-room after scoring 150 runs and go straight to the mirror and start playing his shots. He just stands there, staring at his grip or his back-lift. And he will mutter to himself 'That on-drive wasn't right. It must be straighter. Must get it right. . . .'

Or his head wasn't right. Or his hands were wrong. He's never satisfied. He could score three hundred in a day and he'd spent half the evening in front of the mirror, putting things right. Colin Cowdrey and Ted Dexter were the same.

Lads love to be around when Dennis is here. He keeps giving them useful tips. David Smith speaks volumes about the way Dennis has helped him in the middle.

John Savage is a stickler about technique and style, and is a solid supporter of the high back-lift which Brearley and Gooch brought into prominence. The Lancashire coach says:

Whenever I see photographs of the great old-timers, they are always standing up straight with their bats held high.

Willie Watson was one of the best batsmen I ever played alongside and he always stood up straight. I laughed at him at first. I used to say, 'Look at that fool'. Then one day he said to me, 'By standing like that I can pick up the length better. It's a great help on bad wickets.'

What he said made sense. I didn't laugh any more. Now a lot of batsmen are standing up straight. It's definitely better than being crouched. Though this style doesn't suit all batsmen, I am always shouting, 'Stand up! Stand up!' It's essential for a batsman to have a good backlift.

Savage, a brilliant off-spinner in his day, still bowls regularly in the nets, though the lads tend to joke about it:

I keep 'pulling' the ball back. Flighting it. They call it the 'string' ball.

They want to know how it is done, so I explain to them that a flighted ball doesn't move out. It goes up and drops like a stone. It beats the batsman through the air. My trick comes in releasing the ball early, before my arm has followed through. It is always hanging up there. It is very difficult to judge.

A lad called Ian Davidson has just come on the staff and he spins the ball a mile. It's a bit of a thrill for me trying to polish him up.

When I coach a lad I always say 'Keep spinning it. Keep spinning it.' I don't care where the ball goes. I never say 'Stop, let's have more accuracy.'

In my day we had two seamers in the side, and after they had done their stint I would be on before lunch. And it would be my job to bowl until the next day, when the new ball came round. I was bowling thirty to forty overs a day. A spinner is lucky to bowl that much in a whole match now.

Don Bennett insists that a good action is more important to an orthodox spinner than to any other bowler. He recalls that most of the world's top spinners had a classic action, particularly Fred Titmus, who was his favourite. The shrewd Middlesex coach says:

Fred's greatest asset was that he always wanted to bowl. You could call him out at midnight and he would still have a smile if you had ten overs for him to bowl. And Fred was never beaten. The wicket could be green, brown, red or blue. Fred didn't care. He just loved to bowl.

Whenever I speak to young bowlers I always recall how Titmus loved to be alone in the nets. He spent hours on his own. He put little targets down on the ground for length and line, and he just bowled at the stumps. He used to say, 'I want to see where the ball is landing.'

Titmus started out as a seamer. He swung the ball. Then he came out of the RAF and we played Essex at Westcliff. We had four seamers in the side that day and Fred finished up with one for a hundred. Then as we walked off he said, 'I don't like the look of this. I've had enough.' And he changed to off-spin overnight. He was such a natural spinner that he ended that season with a hundred wickets.

Fred was a cute old boy. When he bowled his spinners, the ball drifted away. So on a good wicket, when the ball didn't turn, it just carried on. He gave batsmen hell. Fred could bowl three different types of delivery. He always had a chance of dismissing a batsman on either side of the wicket.

Titmus was the best for me, though I rate John Emburey very highly. At one stage I thought he would be better than Fred, and he has come very close.

In time, Emburey might well be as good as Titmus. Both were blessed with good cricket brains, and that is so important. Both have varied their pace well. They have confused batsmen. Spin is important, but change of pace is more important still. It gets a batsman in two minds. Flight, to me, is not lobbing the ball up in the air. It is the variation of pace – tricking the batsman into playing early or late.

I remember when Emburey came to us he had a long delivery stride which meant he couldn't make the ball bounce like Titmus. I watched him closely and said, 'You must stand up straighter. You must shorten your stride.'

He did, and he improved.

If players need to work at their game I would advise them to do it out of season. There is a danger that if a player experiments during the season he will fill his head with all sorts of strange ideas and miss the important matters when it comes to the match itself. Players should never take a load of theories into a game if they can avoid it.

Imagine the scene . . . Garfield Sobers and Graham Wiltshire are walking between the twelfth and thirteenth greens on a quiet golf course near Bristol.

Irons and clubs are the order of the day but, as Wiltshire recalls, their conversation inevitably turns to batting, bowling and sunny Barbados:

Gary puts down his bag, lights a cigar, and looking across at me says, 'I'll let you into a secret. I'll tell you why the Caribbean turns out so many brilliant cricketers. . . . It's all balls.'

'Balls?' I exclaimed.

Gary smiled. 'Tennis balls, man. Tennis balls.'

'Oh. . . .'

Gary went on and on about the way the West Indians learn to play their cricket with tennis balls. I hadn't thought of it before. But everything he said made sense.

A few years later I went with our county side to Barbados and studied the West Indian lads at close range. Gary was right. They nearly all played with tennis balls. They didn't need pads or gloves. They just grabbed a piece of wood, rolled out a steel drum and played in the streets. 'Test matches' were taking place around every corner. Back in the forties it was the same over here. You would see three matches in the same street. Now our roads are crammed with cars and lorries.

What impressed me most about the West Indian lads was their confidence. Of course, a tennis ball doesn't hurt. Even the youngest batsman was standing firm against the fastest bowling. When these lads grow up and come to play with a leather ball they will merely regard it as an object. They won't back away.

Seymour Nurse, the great Test batsman of the fifties, met me there and made the point that a tennis ball builds up a lad's coordination, especially when it is thrown against a wall. It was a useful tip and so simple to use.

Some people may say that Wiltshire could have done with this advice way back in his playing days when Gloucestershire were so well-stocked with good bowlers, like George Lambert and Colin Scott, that he found it impossible to command a regular place. Looking back, he says:

I became the permanent twelfth man. The best headwaiter in the business, though I now regard it as the finest thing that ever happened to me. When you're twelfth man you end up talking to all the great players, past and present, sitting around the pavilion. There's a lot of time to pass. So you sit with the opposition and play a listening game.

I gained experience just by listening to great men who could point out what players were doing wrong. It broadened my education. And though I didn't know it then, it prepared the way for my career as a coach.

We used to travel by train in those days. There were always three compartments. One for sleeping, one for playing cards, and one for those who just wanted to chat. I was always with the natterers. I just couldn't learn enough about the game and the people in it.

Even now, when I tell my players to work at their game, I stress that this doesn't mean being in the nets twenty-four hours a day. Working at your game means thinking about it. Deciding on the shots that bring you runs or cause problems. Learning to reduce mistakes and tighten up.

I shall never forget the day I played for the Duke of Beaufort's Eleven against a Gloucestershire side and Wally Hammond came to watch. He was about 57 then and I remember Roly Jenkins, surely one of the best leg-spinners ever to play for England, going up to the great man and saying, 'By the way, sir, I would be very pleased if you could watch my bowling today. And if you see anything wrong, perhaps you could tell me how to correct it.'

Wally had a wonderful temperament. Before he went out to bat he would sit with one glove on, and one glove off. He would smoke cigarette after cigarette. When the time came for him to go to the wicket, he would put his cigarette down and leave it burning. Then the rest of the team would wait for his signal. If he stayed for five minutes and started to twirl his bat, they knew he was there for a long spell. So they put the cigarette out and returned to the dressing-room.

Wally Hammond's genius was admired wherever cricket was played, and Stewart Storey refers to the great man when comparing modern-day fielding techniques to what was considered effective tactics forty years ago.

The Sussex coach says:

Tactics have changed altogether. Wally Hammond, for instance, loved to stroke the ball through the covers and bowlers kept feeding him there. They bowled to his strength, waiting for him to make a mistake and be caught. Now they bowl to a batsman's weakness.

Of all the fine players to represent Sussex in the past ten years none has disappointed them more than the enigmatic Paul Parker, once heralded as a gifted batsman with a guaranteed Test future.

Sadly, Parker's potential has never been realised, and his brilliance has only been seen in flashes. Stewart Storey explains what he sees as the reasons for Parker's stagnation:

Paul has been through a crisis in himself and with his technique. While at Cambridge, and when he first came here, he played and scored runs in a carefree manner.

He had all the credentials to reach the top, but this led to pressure being put on him. If a player comes from university he definitely has a clear start. I hate to say that, but it's a very real fact.

Then Paul started to question what he was doing. He became introspective. He started to analyse the way he played. He began to blind himself with science instead of just getting on with his natural game. And the moment he started to question his technique, something went out of his play.

On his day Paul can murder any bowling attack because he is so enormously strong. He is extremely fast on his feet, and he has a terrific eye.

It is no secret that Paul's problem is settling down early in an innings. He becomes tense. His technique is definitely wanting in that respect. He was lbw eight times in his first twelve innings in 1983. He lost form so badly that we had to drop him. Then he went into the second team and hit two hundreds. So we brought him back into the county side, but nothing had changed. He was still nervy, so we were back where we started.

No matter how much practice a player puts in at the nets, it can never truly compare with what takes place on the square. This is where the men are separated from the boys. It's in the middle that pressure builds up.

Paul feels pressure. He is highly-strung. Very nervy. And all that tension is transferred into a series of convulsive, jerky movements with the bat. Having been a perfectly straight player in the nets, he goes into the middle and plays across the line. This is very much a matter of confidence. So we must get him to relax. We must have a plan for him to play the first dozen balls. When he survives that early pressure he is very likely to make a big score.

A winter of self-analysis between 1983 and '84 seasons, saw Paul go back to the basic parts of his game and by sheer dedication brought about a transformation in his approach to batting. I have the highest admiration for his self-motivation and his will to succeed.

Even the best batsmen slip into bad habits. Their backlift, grip, or maybe the way they move their feet, are the usual problems. Something very basic.

When I mention these things, most of them listen. It's the Smart Alecs who know it all. More and more young professionals are missing out now on the wealth of tips experienced players could be passing down to them simply because they are too pig-headed to pay attention.

Having missed a winter tour himself, David Gibson knew better than most people how Alan Butcher felt when left out of the 1982–83 England party that played in Australia and New Zealand.

In Gibson's case a bad knee injury prevented his trip whereas Butcher was left behind because the selectors finally decided that he was not the man they wanted.

Speaking frankly, Gibson explains why he is convinced that Butcher benefited more by staying at home than if he had gone:

Of course it was a big disappointment to him, but I honestly believe it was a blessing in disguise, because his technique needed attention. We were worried about him flicking at the ball when playing backfoot shots into the covers. He was short of power in that area because his hands weren't working properly.

So we spent the winter in the nets sorting this out. There were some tough sessions, too, but it all paid off and he looked very impressive at the end. He is a much better player for staying at home. The selectors did him a favour.

Butcher would also have gained some comfort from being just one of three shortlisted Surrey players who missed that tour. David Thomas and Jack Richards were also left behind.

Thomas had thrust himself into contention with a series of good all-round displays that ended with a brilliant Man of the Match performance in Surrey's annihilation of Warwickshire in the 1982 NatWest Final. Improvement with the bat and a consistently high standard of wicketkeeping made sure Richards remained under the selectors' eyes right to the time the party was picked. Whether Thomas was ready remains debatable. Gibson says he was not, because certain features of his play still needed to be tightened up:

As a batsman David tends to get himself square-on.

Fortunately for him he has a tremendous eye. He can pick up a short-pitched delivery and whack it out of sight. He hits the ball very hard. He would do even better if he hit it a little straighter. He must learn to play the ball through mid-on.

Cricket is a difficult game, and some players contrive to make it impossible by over-complicating everything they do.

As a bowler, David is beginning to learn how to swing the ball into the right-hander which should make him a big wicket-taker once he has mastered the skill.

He is the ideal chap to have in the dressing-room. He has a lot of 'bottle' and is very quick-witted. Whenever we get turned over he's usually the guy who lifts us off the floor.

Of the players he has discovered and helped during his time as Surrey coach, Gibson is particularly impressed by those senior players who hit bad patches and have the good sense to sort out their errors. Roger Knight was one of these:

Roger suddenly found that he couldn't drive straight, and because it worried him so much I decided to take a close look at the way he played the shot out in the middle. I soon noticed that as he struck the ball his head was actually pointing towards mid-wicket. He was nowhere near the correct line. So when he came back to the dressing-room I suggested he should consider hitting the ball over mid-off.

This surprised him and he said, 'I can't do that.'

'Of course you can,' I said.

So once winter came we went to the indoor nets and looked at his technique in detail. The first thing I saw was that his bottom hand was taking over when he played the problem shot, and this was causing him to pull across the line. Roger worked hard at rectifying the trouble and by the time the season arrived he was hitting brilliantly over mid-off, and perfectly straight.

Many leading batsmen, England players included, get themselves out by hitting across the line. Most of them because they don't give batting enough thought. Their brains are sloppy. All too often you will see even the best player relaxing after forty-five minutes and thinking, 'I'm in now.' That's when they are most vulnerable. Batsmen are never in! There is never a time to relax. Concentration must be kept at a peak all the time if a batsman is to build a big innings. Ken Barrington was a magnificent example of that.

Monte Lynch is a tremendously exciting player, but he's driven us mad. He's always had a marvellous range of attacking shots, but week after week he kept getting himself out too early. He didn't know when to hit and when not to hit. He would slog at his second ball and every stump would be knocked down. He would stick his head in the air and take a mighty swing. He kept throwing his wicket away. Then in the second innings he would put his head down and score sixty or more.

Monte wanted to play all his shots in one over. That was his trouble. And that was crazy. A batsman must never go out looking to take the bowlers on. So we told him about it. We assured him that he had the ability to be a great player, but that he would never make it until he calmed down and learnt to assemble an innings.

Improvement was slow at first, but then the penny seemed to drop. He finally realised that his flamboyant attitude was responsible for the way he was getting out. So he worked hard to become a more consistent player by increasing his concentration, and when he finished top of the club's averages with 1,558 runs in 1983, he had proved that application does produce results. In fact Monte became a much sought-after player and toured South Africa with the so-called West Indian Rebel team.

I'm a great believer in letting players do exactly what comes naturally to them, though I always impress on batsmen that every time they hit the ball in the air they take the chance of being caught. Hitting the ball safely in the air is as much a skill as cutting or driving.

Some players, of course, concentrate on perfecting one specific shot. It may be the square-drive or the hook. Micky Stewart was a great hooker, though some people thought he overdid the shot. They said it kept getting him out.

So Micky went away and considered it, and soon decided that this was a main run-getter. If he played it less, or stopped it altogether, he might not score enough runs to keep his place.

Batsmen come under a lot of unseen pressure out in the

middle. Not least from those close fielders who can't stop talking. In my time it was usually good-humoured banter. Today it can be nasty and crude. Sometimes a batsman does well not to lash out at the man at short-leg and forget all about the ball.

Glamorgan's Wilfred Wooller was one of the best wind-up merchants I ever met. I remember playing at Cardiff and John Edrich was timing every shot perfectly. He had raced to his fifty when Wooller looked up and called to Parkhouse in the gully, 'Do you know, Gilbert, that's the first one to come off the middle all morning!' I liked that. It was funny. But it's not the type of mild comment you are likely to hear today.

On the vast subject of technique, Basil d'Oliveira admits to being perplexed, and is not entirely sure that coaching is the best way to get results:

When I started to play, cricket to me was nothing more than a ball that was used to hit stumps, and a long piece of wood that was used to hit the ball. There was no science. Nothing complicated. I knew nothing about movement or swing, or the best technical way to cut or drive.

Sometimes I wonder whether it is a good thing to know too much. The game was simple to me in those early days. Very basic.

When I first came to England from South Africa I went into the nets with Middleton in the Lancashire League and found the ball moving around in a way I had never known before. We had a chap called Roger Clarkson who could swing the ball like Bob Massie, the Australian. He was fantastic in the nets, but could never put it together in the middle. He bamboozled me. The shots I had played all my life were suddenly letting me down. I kept hitting the ball in the air. So I thought 'What the hell am I doing here?'

To make it worse, I had never seen a green wicket before. I was terrible. After five weeks of sheer hell Eric Price, the former Lancashire and Essex left-armer, said to me, 'Look, Basil, it's time we put this right.'

So he took me aside and explained why I was lifting the ball so often. He pointed out that I was still playing the South African way. I was hitting the ball as it came onto the bat. He then explained that in England the ball doesn't come on like that. It pitches and stops. So I was playing too early and being caught in the covers or at mid-off.

Tips like that were a great help. It was the same with my bowling. They made me bowl cutters on a matting wicket in South Africa but when I came to England I was always too short. The ball kept going away at right angles.

What I learned in those days, I am passing on now. When lads bowl short or down the wrong line, I must know why. I must be able to correct them.

There seems little doubt in d'Oliveira's mind that many players might learn more by exchanging ideas than by endless hours of practical tuition in a tedious net:

Sometimes a player might offer advice. If he does, then listen closely – that's what I tell my lads.

I remember once going through a terrible spell. It went on for a fortnight. I couldn't tell what was wrong. Tom Graveney was batting with me, but even he couldn't help. All he could say was 'You are playing well enough, Basil, but you are not getting runs. You're having a lean time. Just keep going.' But I didn't see it that way. Deep inside I knew there was something definitely wrong. I was worried.

Then Worcester went to play Surrey at The Oval, and I asked Tom if he would come with me to the nets early next morning. By the time I had padded up I noticed Surrey's wicket-keeper Arthur McIntyre walking around the ground. Arthur was a great judge of a player, and Tom said, 'Why don't you have a word with him, Bas?'

So when Arthur reached the back of the net, I said, 'Would you mind taking a look at me? I'm not happy with the way I am playing.'

'What's the problem?' he said. 'I've noticed in the papers that you've not been getting many runs lately.' He then told me to go on batting and that he would walk around the ground and keep an eye on me.

Fifteen minutes later he came back and stopped behind the net. He said, 'The only thing I can see, Bas, is that you are looking at your boots when you play your shots.'

I stopped and thought about it. He was right. When a

batsman is playing well, he looks up the wicket. He follows the ball. But I wasn't. I was so concerned about not getting out that I was looking down at my bootlaces and trapping the ball.

Arthur was spot on. And he and Surrey soon paid for putting me right. I went straight out and hit a hundred!

Then a short time later I went to Pakistan with England, and Roger Prideaux was with us and he went through a terrible patch. I watched him closely and he was doing exactly what I had done. When we returned to England we were both picked for the MCC team to play at Lord's and on the night before the match we went out for a few drinks. Roger was a good batsman, but he said to me, 'Bas, I can't get runs these days. I just don't know what's wrong.'

I told him he had the problem that nearly drove me mad. And as the tour had gone on he had kept putting more and more pressure on himself. Then I told him how Arthur McIntyre had put me right and Roger went out and became a new man.

It's strange, but if golfers find something wrong with their game they go straight back to their coaches. Nicklaus, Palmer and Watson are always doing that. The same applies in tennis. Borg, Connors, Navratilova, they all have personal coaches, and they all use them. But I can count on the fingers of one hand the number of times a county player has come back and said, 'I think this is wrong. Can you help?'

We have a brilliant young fielder in Tim Curtis. He excelled for me in the second team. Then he went into our county side, and Glenn Turner came to me one day and said, 'This lad Tim Curtis isn't much of a fielder, is he?'

'Don't be silly,' I said. 'Of course he is. He's one of the best we've got.'

'Well, he's not in the first team,' said Glenn.

Next day I stopped Tim and said, 'How are you getting on? I hear your fielding isn't too good.'

'That's strange, Basil, but you're right,' he said. 'I don't seem to be going into the ball. I seem to be hesitating. I think I'm scared of making a mistake.'

What he said made sense. I teach all my players to attack in the field. To go to the ball. But if Glenn hadn't said anything, Tim would have carried on, despite knowing that he was doing something wrong. He had no plans to mention it to me. That's what I find annoying.

As a player I used to watch other players in a certain way, but now as a coach, I look for different things. If I am watching a bowler, I will put my binoculars on him for an hour or more. I'll study his run-up, the height of his arm, his follow-through and whether he falls away as he bowls the ball. I will watch him in every stride until he pulls up. I will watch him and no one else. Unless I watch him from the start to finish, I know I will learn nothing.

Many bowlers who come in from the Leagues don't have length or line. In club cricket they can get away with it because of their pace or spin, but not in County Cricket. So I give them a net and tell them I want two overs of hitting the off stump. It gets their concentration going.

Then, when I look at a batsman, the thing I want to know most is how he plays the ball. All good batsmen play under their noses. They let the ball come on to them. Once a batsman can play this way, he has the basis on which to prosper.

A lot of batsmen are affected mentally by the game. They cram so much into their minds that they can't think clearly. When I look at certain batsmen in the middle, I know they are 'in'. I know a nuclear war wouldn't shift them. But then I look at others and I can tell that in five overs they'll be back in the pavilion. So I say to our young players, 'Take guard, relax, feel comfortable.'

All too often a batsman is wound up like a spring. He can be there 75 minutes and his score is only 28. And that's when I worry. That's the danger period. Between 28 and 35. That's when the concentration goes. Between 36 and 48, they are usually fine. They have 50 on their minds, and they apply themselves to reach it. Between 65 and 78 is another danger time. Beyond that they are usually great. They start grafting towards their hundred. The best batsmen, of course, keep their concentration up for every ball right through an innings, but there are not many of them around.

My advice to batsmen is 'Talk to yourself. Keep nattering.' You can't be locked up for it. And to bowlers I say, 'Set a batsman up for two or three overs ahead. Then slip one down the leg side. If he takes a whack he has fallen into your trap'.

D'Oliveira's call for greater concentration on the field is echoed loudly two hundred miles away at Taunton by Somerset's Peter Robinson:

Concentration is vital to all batsmen. Good players teach themselves to do it. Just as they teach themselves to play the hook or the cover-drive. No batsman will succeed unless he is able to concentrate over long periods. It is something no coach can teach.

The county championship is particularly hard because players have to grind away day after day. That's where Viv Richards is so special. When he goes to the wicket you feel he's going to stay there and score a hundred. He knows how to bat for a day. Tom Graveney and John Edrich were like that. They could set themselves up for a big innings.

People often ask me to compare Tom with Viv. It's not easy. Viv is a destroyer. Tom was a stylist. A butcher and surgeon if you like. Viv hits the ball out of the ground whereas Tom preferred to caress it over the ropes. When Tom scored a hundred you had to look up at the scoreboard to confirm that it was done. You would think 'Oh, God, he's got a hundred.' As a bowler you wouldn't feel he had taken you apart. But when Viv scores a hundred you feel it. You know he's ripped you to pieces. Tom's record was fantastic, and so will Viv's be when he decides to retire.

I use that comparison butcher and surgeon because I remember my uncle Roly Jenkins referring to the famous West Indian pair Worrell and Weekes in the same way. He reckoned Weekes was the butcher while Worrell was the surgeon. Brute force coupled with elegance. A devastating combination.

When seeking that special player of the future, Colin Page says he always looks hard at a boy's technique, his temperament, and his powers of concentration. Of technique, the strapping Kent coach says:

A player must be allowed to develop his own personal style. When I coach eight- and nine-year-olds I stick strictly to the book. But as the boys grow older and show different aptitudes, I merely polish them up. I am horrified when I hear people actually coaching out a player's strong point because it doesn't conform exactly to the advice laid down in the textbook.

If a player can hit fours while standing on his head, then only a fool would stop him. Being unorthodox is not a sin. Take Simon Hinks for example. People keep telling me that he won't last because he hits the ball in the air. Yet Simon and I both know that if he stopped hitting the ball that way he would be removing his greatest asset. He would have little else going for him.

Simon loves to hammer the bad ball, and because of that he will always be a crowd-pleaser. Of course, to become a regular first-team player he must hit the ball in safe areas. And that's where the skill and discipline come in.

Too many coaches, I'm sorry to say, stick rigidly to the textbook. With toddlers that might be all right, but there is no way a coach can follow the same principles at county level. He has to be flexible. He has to allow for all sorts of different techniques. Often it's doing the unorthodox well that turns an average player into a world-class superstar.

People say that all great batsmen stand absolutely still until the ball leaves the bowler's hand. Well, Colin Cowdrey didn't, and he could bat a bit. When Colin faced a very fast bowler it was not unusual to see him move slightly across his stumps at the point of delivery. In that way he found he was in the perfect position to play the very quick ball. It worked beautifully for him, though in club cricket, where the bowling is not so fast, I would advise batsmen to remain totally still until the ball is bowled.

Peter Sainsbury sees it in exactly the same way. Only when the bowling is extremely fast does he approve of a batsman moving before the ball is released:

It's a matter on which I am very strict. Some players will insist that they don't move, so when I go to the nets I catch them out. I tell the bowler to run up, stop at the stumps, and to keep the ball in his hand. Then, when the batsman moves, I just smile down the wicket at him. I don't need to say a word.

Obviously there are times when I have to break this rule.

That's what's great about cricket. You need to adapt and be flexible. Should a batsman be facing a very fast bowler then it might be to his advantage to move very slightly just as the ball is being delivered.

If you watch carefully you will see that most of the world's best batsmen either move back or across their stumps. Some even push their front foot forward as the ball is being bowled. Viv Richards does. But usually only against the genuine quick bowler.

Though Yorkshire's ebullient left-hand batsman Kevin Sharp is not always absolutely technically correct, he is still extremely productive, and his coach Doug Padgett has no desire to change him:

To alter a lad like Kevin, who is a little unorthodox, could get him into a dreadful tangle. That's when a coach has to be so careful. To mess around with a player's technique when he is doing perfectly well is utterly wrong, dangerous, and stupid. But there are people around who can't resist the opportunity to meddle.

A good coach will know what to leave alone, even though the lad may not be playing in the way the purists admire.

The same applies to bowlers. If a lad can move the ball it doesn't matter one bit if his action isn't all poetry in motion. If he can bowl well despite a poor action, then you let him carry on. It's what happens at the other end that matters. Where the ball pitches, and what it does.

Kevin went through a lean patch in the early 1980s and people questioned his temperament. The truth is, he lost confidence. He became unsure of himself.

There is no substitute for confidence in this game. Once a lad knows how to play cricket, confidence can be a tremendous asset. If you think you're going to do well, that's half the battle. If you feel good as you go out to bat or when running up to bowl, you will do much better than the fellow who is all on edge, even if he has a little more ability.

Every player goes through a bad spell at sometime during his career. My job is to reassure that chap that he is still a good player. That things are going against him. To make him stick to his principles, and not to start thinking of changing his game.

Now that Bill Athey has gone to Gloucester I can see Kevin developing into a good batsman. He feels more secure these days. He knows he's going to get an extended run no matter how well he plays. He no longer feels his future depends entirely on one innings. That he must get a big score or he's out. That's pressure.

I've known Kevin since he was a schoolboy, and he's always scored runs. I suppose he's given the impression of being nervous because he fidgets at the crease, but he's no worse than anyone else. Some people just show it more than others. Everyone who plays this game is a bit apprehensive until he gets some runs on the board.

Kevin Lyons stresses the point that cricket, for all its technical attributes and gross imperfections, is a game that is totally based on scoring runs, and he makes a loud appeal for more attention to be paid to quick singles:

The object of batting is to score runs. That's why the quick single is such an art. I coach a group of lads in Cape Town, and if they run without calling, I give them out.

A lot of England's best players are run out, not because they are slow between the wickets, but because they are bad judges.

If nothing else, the one-day games have demanded that all batsmen should improve their running. Pinching singles is a skill – the most under-rated part of batting. There are some bowlers a batsman can never hit, so stealing singles is essential for him to keep the score ticking along.

This urgent demand to score runs often ends in a batsman developing and then over-using a 'favourite shot'. The hook and square-cut are the two most commonly seen and frequently cause that batsman's downfall.

Peter Sainsbury approaches the subject carefully:

Before I suggest that a batsman stops playing a dangerous shot I study first how many runs he is scoring from it, because batting is all about percentages.

I remember someone once saying to Roy Marshall, 'If you didn't play that square-cut so often in the early part of your innings you'd be at the crease a lot longer.'

And Roy replied, 'But that's where I get my runs. If I dropped that shot altogether, I'd hardly ever score.'

139

Alan Oakman endorses all that is said about protecting the unorthodox player and recalls John Whitehouse's peculiar stance as the perfect example:

It was terrible. Everything was wrong about it, especially his left shoulder pointing to mid-on. Yet it wasn't until he started to bat that way that his runs began to flow. That's the beauty of cricket. You can be very unorthodox but still be successful. Not every batsman stands in the way advised by the technical experts, but we don't want them to. All we want are results.

Batsmen always have it best. There is no argument about that. When a batsman scores a hundred the public will have watched it right through. But when a bowler takes six wickets he usually accumulates them in two or three spells, and what he achieves tends to go unnoticed.

Batsmen also last longer. They suffer less wear and tear. And batting has its rewards. It has honour and glory. All bowlers end up with are blisters and backache.

For some peculiar reason it seems that whenever the subject of technique is raised, the problems are invariably related to batting. It's as though technique has no place in a bowler's world. This, of course, is not true, as England paceman Neil Foster will confirm — and he has the scars to prove it.

Foster had two silver plates stitched in his back to repair the wear and tear of a delivery action that threatened to put him out of the game. Both plates have now been removed and, using a new technique, Foster has become a front-line force in the England attack.

As a qualified coach, Foster knows only too well what caused his injury and he's discussed it at length with his Essex colleague and coach Ray East, who says:

Neil's injury occurred because he kept leaning back towards mid-off just as he was about to bowl. He hollowed his back in the delivery stride which put too much pressure on his spine. Tony Pigott, of Sussex, and Dennis Lillee have had the same trouble. It's a common problem among quick bowlers. After a time they find their spine cannot absorb the pressure.

When Neil came back after the operation we watched him bowl at the indoor school. We filmed him from every angle and then played it back in slow motion. To everyone's delight, he was leaning back properly.

Since then Neil has worked extremely hard to get a good line and to bowl close to the stumps. He is determined to make batsmen play at every ball. By the time he is twenty-seven, he should be bowling at top speed. Records show that this is the age when most quick bowlers come to their peak.

Foster's rapid transition from schoolboy to adult came appropriately when Essex were blooding wicketkeeper David East, the man who now has to cope with the young bowler's thunderbolts.

Though born nearby in London, it was as a Northamptonshire reject that East arrived at Essex, saying he would like to try his luck as deputy to Neil Smith.

Ray East, who is not related to David, assesses his wicketkeeper:

After seeing him in the nets we agreed to give him a one-year contract, though mainly as a batsman. Bob Richards, my assistant coach, and our reserve wicketkeeper for many years, decided to take David under his wing. He spent a lot of time with him. It usually takes a wicketkeeper to judge a wicketkeeper.

Bob sets a very high standard and he thought David was a bit flashy at first and that he didn't catch the ball often enough. Encouraged by Bob's enthusiasm, David worked hard in the nets and played in our second team. I remember Bob saying 'He's got that awful habit of letting his hands hang at his sides as he bends down.' Bob then helped him to put it right and once he got into our first team he began to take any number of one-handed diving catches. Our seam bowlers were delighted with him.

Strangely enough, David is left-handed, Bob was left-handed, and our young wicketkeeper Neil Burns is also left-handed. Perhaps that explains why they are all so good down the legside.

Bob reckons very few county players know a lot about wicketkeeping. He says many of them have recommended wicketkeepers to him, but when he's gone to see these lads they've turned out to be rubbish. Over the years I have noticed that wicketkeepers always talk to wicketkeepers. David often goes up to Bob and asks him to watch whenever he can.

If David had an early problem, it was standing up to the spin bowlers. This is the hardest part of a wicketkeeper's game. David Acfield caused a few problems at first. He is very clever with his flight and spin. He was not only beating the batsmen, but fooling David as well. Once David learned to watch Acfield's hand, his confidence grew. He stands up well now.

When David first came into the side, Bob thought he had too many mannerisms. He kept adjusting his pads, tapping his gloves, moving his cap, and hopping up and down. He wasted a lot of energy. They were all unnecessary movements. Keeping wicket for more than a hundred overs on a hot day eventually sorted that out.

Chris Gladwin is another young Essex player whose phenomenal start has already stamped him as a batsman with a long and exciting future. As opening partner to Graham Gooch perhaps it's only natural that he loves to explode and whack the ball at the slightest opportunity.

At face value there seems little wrong in a powerful batsman exuding aggression and trying to hit the skin off the ball, but Ray East, in his role as a cautious coach, also sees the dangers:

It must be said that playing his shots could have been Chris's downfall. When he came on the staff he was too eager to open up. We had to work hard to discipline his batting. He tended to hit the ball in the air towards the covers, and he went through one terrible spell when he was caught there time and again. He was even out that way when batting for Young England against the West Indians.

He knew it had to stop if he was going to be a county player, and that's where practising at our indoor school helped him a lot. He came in day after day and worked hard, and now he rarely hits the ball in the air on the off side.

Chris's trouble came from trying to drive the ball that was too short. He wasn't judging the length correctly. And we also told him not to shut the bat on quick bowlers, but to let it come through.

Before Chris can establish himself as a front-line batsman he must realise that scores of thirty are not enough.

The difference between first and second-team bowling is that in championship cricket the ball is usually straight. County bowlers are difficult to score off, and that's where a batsman's temperament comes in. He must know how to build an innings.

With so much quick bowling these days, especially in Test matches, it can be difficult for a batsman to attack. My advice to those playing on the back foot is never to attack unless the ball is below the height of the bails. If it's any higher you would be wise to defend. In this way the shot will not be played with bat being pushed away from the body.

Several of our English batsmen forgot this theory when facing Lillee, Hogg and Lawson during the 1982 tour of Australia and perished at the crease, presenting catch after catch to slips and wicketkeeper.

Ray East makes the point that as an advanced coach he can demonstrate a shot as well as, say, Graham Gooch:

Standing in a net showing others what to do is no great sweat. The test comes when a bowler is charging in at you and slamming the ball down at sixty miles an hour. Gooch has the skills to play the shots in matches, and that's where I tend to struggle a bit.

Gooch demonstrated all the front-foot shots for the National Cricket Association film sponsored by NatWest. I met him at the launch in London, and he was so impressed he said he would like to take a coaching course!

We encourage all our professional players to take the NCA course once they reach twenty-one. We used to insist that they went straight on to the advanced course, because in that way they can relate to one another. When playing and practising they are talking a common language.

David East has passed with honours, and Pont, Hardie, and Lillie have all gained their advanced certificates. Norbert Philip passed his 'advanced' in the West Indies.

Technique is something we all treat very seriously, and Keith Fletcher is so concerned about his that he plays very little golf in the cricket season. He says that so much 'bottom' hand is needed to swing a club that bad habits can come in and a batsman may find himself skying the ball once he gets to the middle.

On this point, Brian Reynolds totally disagrees:
I shall always remember Gubby Allen telling me at Lord's: 'When you are playing golf, you are playing cricket. The occasional shot comes in both games.'

Most cricketers play golf, and I say 'Fine. Carry on swinging.' Right through my career I found that if my cricket was going well, my golf was good. And when my cricket was bad, my golf was bad. It's all about timing.

To reach county level and then survive, a player will require a great deal more than technique. A sound, calm temperament is another invaluable asset, a strength which Colin Page defines as a gift. He says:
When a player says he is not nervous, and he means it, then it's probably time for him to quit. I have seen players physically sick before they go out to bat, and it's nothing to be ashamed of. And I have seen countless players sit for hours, all padded up, waiting their turn, and smoking cigarette after cigarette until the butt-ends are coming up over their ankles.

What I like to see more than anything else is a batsman who yawns. Then I really know that he is nervous. I know he is ready for the job in hand.

The early success of Paul Prichard is yet another feather in the cap for Essex, whose superb organisational skills keep yielding a plethora of home-grown talent. Just nineteen, Prichard has already confirmed the promise he showed as a schoolboy, to the delight of his coach Ray East:
Paul forced his way into our first team after a string of good scores in the Second Eleven. He made his championship debut against Worcestershire and got us out of the mire. He kept calm and stayed there after half the team was back in the pavilion. We were 30 for 4 when he went in, and he pulled us together and scored 86. That proved his temperament was right.

He has always looked a good player ever since he came to

our nets as a thirteen-year-old. Even then we all thought he would play for Essex one day. He's the best lad of that age that I've ever seen. I bowled my hardest at him but I couldn't get him out. His technique against the spinner was uncanny for someone so young. He picked up the length and line with no effort. Everything just came easy to him.

Ray East is clearly happy that Prichard can cope with the pressure that obviously exists every time he goes out to the wicket, though not very talented batsman has this capability, as Ken Higgs confirms:

Pressure can be a major problem. Our Tim Boon suffers from it, which is a shame because he is always so technically correct. He desperately needs to believe in himself.

In the second team he looks a fine player. So we push him up to the first team and he suddenly thinks he has to occupy the crease for a long time to get a big score. Sooner or later he gets the good ball and is out.

So I tell him that if the first ball is a half-volley he should give it the treatment. Happily he has now scored his maiden first-class century and has a few other big scores under his belt. He has more confidence these days, and he should go from strength to strength.

We have five or six players under twenty competing for three places. That makes it hard. Someone has to be disappointed. So I say to them, 'The opportunity is there, you must prove you can take it.'

In addition to temperament and technique, every county coach singles out dedication as yet another vital factor in a cricketer's make-up.

Brian Reynolds: The biggest change in the game now from the time I played is the appalling lack of dedication. County players who don't go abroad in winter should have at least one net a week. Players must be more positive. They don't think enough.

I shall always remember Alec Bedser telling me that it wasn't until he toured Australia and tied up Arthur Morris that he realised he could bowl the leg-cutter. And that was in a Test match. He put his fingers across the ball in a new way and discovered he had a secret weapon, which he then used to dismiss the world's best batsmen right through his career.

Alec was amazed. He had never bowled it before. But he was always experimenting. Always trying something new. It didn't matter to him whether it was the indoor nets in Surrey or a vital Test match in Sydney.

Whenever I have a bowler who is too big for his boots, I usually say, 'Right, so you think you're good. Well, let me tell you about Alec Bedser. . . .' I then recall the morning I batted against him on a green wicket at The Oval. When we went in for lunch I could see every mark on the pitch where the ball had landed. It was a remarkable sight. One page of a tabloid newspaper would have covered the whole lot, except for the few he had dug in short, and the occasional Yorker.

Alec was an expert at keeping the ball on the spot. He was like an old woman – nag, nag, nag. He gave you no respite. Sooner or later, he knew the batsman would get frustrated and make the fatal mistake.

Geoff Boycott is the only player I can think of who might have had the temperament to survive if he had been around then. As a player, I admire Boycott immensely. He's been tremendous. His critics have said that he is selfish. Well, on occasions, that might be so, but ninety-eight per cent of the time when a batsman plays for himself, it is also best for the team. It all goes wrong in the other two per cent. That's when the players see that the batsman doesn't have the team at heart. So they break away from him, and that's when the bad feeling creeps in.

As a coach I am forever seeking ways of helping players to believe in themselves. Some of them are so bad they can drive you to drink – literally! I worry for them. I want them to succeed.

It is a curious fact, but players with exceptional ability often don't appreciate the gifts they have. It's usually those with average ability, and who are dedicated, who keep coming through. They come out far ahead of those with oodles of talent but who won't work at their game.

To make the grade, a cricketer must play as often as he can and practise hard. A batsman must bat, and a bowler must bowl.

7

The overseas invaders

Colin Cowdrey still blushes with embarrassment, it seems, whenever he's asked to recall the day he unwittingly recommended the great Viv Richards to Somerset rather than to his beloved Kent. The story goes that England's majestic hero of the fifties and sixties was soaking up a Caribbean holiday when he accidentally gave a tip to Len Creed, a fanatical Somerset supporter and a man with a keen cricket eye. Creed pricked his ears as Cowdrey extolled the skills of a prolific Antiguan batsman by the name of Isaac Vivian Alexander Richards.

It so happened that Kerry O'Keefe had not returned from Australia, so Somerset had a vacancy for an overseas player. Satisfied that Cowdrey was a reliable judge, Creed made immediate arrangements for the unknown Richards to travel to England. He booked his ticket on an early flight and paid his fare without even seeing a single shot. He took him on trust.

Arriving in Somerset, the precocious Richards joined Landsdown, a club side in the Western League, and Cowdrey's prognostications were soon proved right. Richards had extraordinary talent. He dominated the League and played the occasional second-team game for Somerset to acclimatise himself for the county matches to come.

No one remembers Richards's instant impact better than chief coach Peter Robinson, who says:

Viv's first season was in 1974. He scored 1,200 runs and averaged 33. In those days we used to take an old temporary stand around with us and Viv had to help to put it up. I shall never forget him coming to me and saying, 'I don't want too much of this, man.' Of course he soon became so important that no one dared ask him to lift a spanner in case he damaged himself. He didn't build grandstands for long.

Batting means everything to Viv. I was at Taunton at seven one evening, and who should walk in, but Viv.

'Where the hell have you come from?' I said.

'Barbados, man. Just got off a plane at Heathrow. I've come straight down. Please, can you find a few lads to give me a net?'

I looked at him daft. What an incredible man, I thought. He had just ended a tough Test series in the West Indies, and here he was literally stepping off a plane and asking for a net. Next day wouldn't do. He had to have one then. That's the type of professional he is. I couldn't think of one other player in the world who would have done that. So I took a net and bowled to him, and a few others joined in.

Viv has always said that when a batsman returns to England from the West Indies or Australia he needs to be a yard closer to the ball. His favourite words are, 'Look at my foot, man. Watch my foot.'

He always wants to talk about batting. And he treats a net with great respect. It's serious business to him. He's not one of those who goes in and tries to smash every ball into the river. It's a pleasure to bowl to him.

If he goes wrong, which is not often, he's always willing to take advice. He's a humble man. On a few occasions he has tipped over slightly when playing a shot. So I might say to him, 'You're falling over a bit.'

And he'll say, 'I know, man. I've got to get that right. I must watch that.'

A net will become worn from time to time, but it doesn't matter how badly it plays, you'll never hear Viv complain. Even if it's had a week's cricket on it, he will still go in. He will say, 'Don't worry, man, it's all good practice.'

Then he will merely treat it as a difficult net. As long as he can pad up and bat, Viv is a happy man. I have always admired him for that. And he's a marvellous example for any young player.

In his early days he used to get himself out rather than bowlers beating him. Then the turning-point came in Australia. He had a rough time early on, so he was asked to open. He came back from that tour a very mature player. I think he disciplined his game a bit more, which is so important for a batsman.

He doesn't throw his wicket away now. He builds an innings, especially on the big occasions. We've been to a number of one-day finals and I can always sense the change in him. As we approach the ground I can almost hear him thinking, 'This is it. This is my day.' He thrives on a full house at Lord's. Great entertainers love a large audience. They all want a stage. No matter whether they are batsmen or comedians they love to be out front doing their stuff.

Besides his brilliant batting, Viv is probably the best fielder living. He can catch at slip, at cover, and on the boundary, and his ground fielding is absolute poetry.

He's no fool with the ball, either. Basically he bowls little out-swingers, but he's a lot nippier than most people think.

He's excelled at the one-day game. He's always involved. He doesn't say, 'I'm the best batsman in the world, let someone else get on with the bowling.' Even if he doesn't score a run, he usually takes a couple of wickets and saves around thirty in the field. To be fair, I feel there are times when our supporters are quite happy to see one of our openers dismissed so that Viv can go in.

As with Viv Richards, it was again the mercurial Len Creed who engineered the capture of Joel Garner, the most effective bowler in the world.
Peter Robinson: We desperately needed a quick bowler and Len had heard about this chap Garner who was knocking them over in the Lancashire League. So we signed him.

Joel was on contract to Littleborough and couldn't play for us at weekends. But we decided to be patient and he came to us full time in the end. He's been a terrific success, though he's cost us a packet in hotel bills. At 6ft 7in he's so long that he needs a double bed wherever we go.

No one can argue that Somerset have led the way in recruiting the finest brand of overseas player to supplement their wonderful wealth of homegrown talent.
Besides Richards and Garner, their illustrious list includes Greg Chappell, Sunil Gavaskar, Colin McCool, Bill Alley, Kerry O'Keefe and more recently the formidable Martin Crowe.
Robinson defends this controversial policy:
I don't believe for one minute that it has stopped too many

local players coming through. If lads are good enough they will make their mark no matter who we bring in from abroad.

Just imagine the outcry if I said we were getting rid of Joel and Viv. Membership would drop by thousands. Our problem will come in finding people to replace them. All these players have helped enormously towards our success. Particularly in the one-day games. Our membership has shot up from a regular three thousand to well over six thousand, and it's increasing all the time.

Fed for years on an extravagant diet of Richards and Botham, the Somerset connoisseurs took time to acquire a taste for the more subdued offerings of Martin Crowe. The neat, correct New Zealander took until the second week in June to score his maiden championship century and, if anything, had shown better form with the ball. But once he settled in and became accustomed to the speed of the slower English wickets, the hundreds started to flow.

Looking back, Peter Robinson says:

At first people expected too much of him. They forgot he was still in his early twenties, still very new to the first-class game. He was under pressure. He was following the world's greatest player in Viv Richards, and some people thought he should have been cracking six after six all over the place.

But even in those early days Martin came good at crucial times – in the one-day games, and on bad wickets when everyone else was struggling.

Gavaskar got the call to Somerset for just one season while Richards and Garner were away on Test duty. Robinson says of that solitary summer:

Sunil played a few masterly innings, but never really came to terms with the John Player League. No one expects Gavaskar to hit sixes, but he did strike some beauties over the Taunton Indoor School in a fabulous knock of 120 against Middlesex.

As a coach I found him a treat to watch in the nets. And, like Viv and Joel, he loved to talk about the game. I don't profess to know the lot, so I am always picking brains. Whatever I learn, I pass on. How can I be expected to know as much about batting as Viv? Or more about bowling than Joel?

Roy Marshall, the former Hampshire and West Indian

batsman, is on our cricket committee now. He helps me a lot. He has a pub in Taunton and comes to most of our second team matches.

Roy is a great student of the batting game. He sees things that I might miss. It's good to have someone else's opinion. A coach can work with a player for a long time and see nothing wrong. Then someone new comes on the scene and spots a flaw straightaway. Cricket is a game in which you never stop learning.

Players, pitches and attitudes have changed enormously since Peter Robinson first joined Somerset in 1969. One of his earliest recollections was playing alongside a young, elegant stroke-maker called Greg Chappell:

Greg was just nineteen when I first saw him. He was totally unknown. He had been recommended to us by someone in Australia. He was a gift from the Gods.

What struck me most about Greg was the confidence he had in his own ability. If he hit a problem, he worked it out for himself. I remember he was bowling leg breaks that bordered on the abysmal. Then he saw Bill Alley bowling and he said, 'If that Aussie can bowl like that and get wickets, then so can I.' And he did.

In his second season with us he bowled more than four hundred overs of medium-pace and took forty-five wickets. He learnt to bowl over here, and later on used his skills to good effect for Australia.

Even when he came here he was tremendously strong on the leg side. He hooked well. He scored the first John Player hundred, at an obscure place called Brislington near Bristol. On the previous day we had started a championship match against Surrey, and in the evening had trooped off to the Crown and Sceptre. Intikhab Aslam was there, talking about how he liked to bowl in John Player matches, and then next day Greg murdered him.

Playing in English cricket helped Greg a lot. It has helped Viv, too. Possibly what this country has done over the years is educate the rest of the world. Over here they learn to play on all types of wickets which helps them to master their trade. Wickets were not covered when Greg played for us, which

meant he learned a lot at places like Weston and Bath where
the pitches always helped the bowlers.

*Basil d'Oliveira cleverly detected an obscure problem when
Worcester's young Barbadian Ricky Ellcock first came under his
gaze. Ellcock had just started his second spell and d'Oliveira
noticed the lad was suddenly jaded. There was no bounce in his
run-up and his pace had dropped. D'Oliveira says:*

I noticed that Ricky had bowled magnificently in his first
spell of six overs, but all his fire had gone when he came back.
'That's odd,' I thought. 'What's happening here?' And he
said, 'I don't know what it is, but I feel I am seizing up. My
whole body seems to go stiff.' I spoke to the physio about it.
And he said to me, 'Basil, I think this chap is losing salt. West
Indians tend to perspire a lot. I think he's stiffening up.'

Next morning we called Ricky in and put him on a course of
salt tablets and the problem was solved.

When I have a young player like Ricky, I always want him
to watch the best. So when Malcolm Marshall came here with
Hampshire, I told Ricky, 'Just sit there all day and watch this
bloke.'

Marshall bowled beautifully. He bowled us out. And he
didn't bowl one bouncer. He just kept the ball up, moved it
about and was quick. 'There you are', I said. 'That's what
you've got to learn. That's what's going to come with a lot of
hard work.' And I said to him, 'Tonight, when you've got
time, grab hold of him. Have a word with him.'

I can still see them now, standing at the bar, chatting like
old buddies. Marshall told him what I had told him. Too
many quick bowlers grab the new ball and have five slips,
three gullys and a fine leg. Everyone is close in. They have no
cover, no mid-off and no mid-on. Marshall said, 'Don't be
embarrassed, man. Bowl with a mid-off and a mid-on. Have a
cover-point. Then you can pitch the ball up. You won't be
afraid of being driven. You'll only take wickets if you pitch the
ball up.'

Having come from the West Indies, Ricky will probably
take two to three years to bowl an English length. All the West
Indians tend to bowl a yard short when they come here first.
On the quicker West Indian wickets batsmen can hit through

the line of the ball and over the top. It's the same in Australia.
So the bowlers must keep the ball a bit short.

*All through his career d'Oliveira maintained the utmost respect for
West Indian cricketers, and none more than Gary Sobers, whom he
still rates as the best player he ever saw.*

No matter who was bowling, Sobers always had enormous
time to play the ball. He was a great back-foot player. I
could count on the fingers of one hand the number of times
I saw him hit on the pads. He could have played without
them.

I do remember one Test when Ray Illingworth got the ball
past Gary's bat several times. So in the evening I said to him,
'Gary, I see Illy got you playing and missing quite a bit out
there today. What was wrong?' And he looked at me and said,
'Basil, I think you must get it right. I was not playing and
missing. He was missing me! It was his job to get the edge of
my bat. But he didn't.'

Only Gary could speak that way. He used to say, 'Give me
the right ball and I will swing it and seam it on any wicket in
the world.' Gary argued that all movement, both through the
air and off the pitch, depended entirely on the state of the ball.
He was adamant that swing had nothing to do with the wicket
or the atmosphere, or even the sweat from the bowler's brow.

*Ellcock is the latest in the long line of Worcester's adopted sons,
none of whom made a bigger impression than Glenn Turner,
though, as d'Oliveira points out, Turner was far from being an
instant success when he arrived from New Zealand.*

When Glenn came here, he couldn't hit the ball off the
square. But he stayed there. His sole intention was to remain
at the crease.

Technically he did well. For a long time he really believed
that no one could get him out. It wasn't the bowler who got
him out, he got himself out. At times Glenn was quite selfish,
but that selfishness usually helped the whole team, so we
didn't mind too much.

Glenn didn't talk a lot about the game down here. He didn't
pass on a lot of knowledge to other people. He was a bit of a
loner really.

Strangely enough, in his last two seasons with us he became an entirely different man. He realised there were other things to life besides playing cricket. Once the John Player started he had to hit the ball hard or be left out. So he released himself from the shackles of just living purely to collect runs. He blossomed, and we all know how well he was playing at the finish.

Seeing that I was an overseas player myself, people expect me to keep quiet on the subject, but I have very definite views on it. I think one overseas player to a county is enough. No side should need more than that. But we must not stop them altogether. County cricket must not become so small-minded that we can't have sixteen of the world's best players in our competition.

During the past fifteen winters of coaching in South Africa, the lucky Kevin Lyons has had the opportunity of spotting the very best players even before they leave school. Loyal to his county back home, Lyons has then confidently tipped off Glamorgan about the emerging stars, only to be told, time and time again, that their services were not required.

It was while coaching in Johannesburg that Lyons first saw Allan Lamb, Peter Kirsten and Garth Le Roux. A trio of players with exceptional talent.

All three were in their teens, and Lyons was so impressed he excitedly recommended them to Glamorgan. But, for reasons never disclosed, Glamorgan showed no interest.

Kirsten eventually joined Derbyshire, Le Roux signed for Sussex, and the majestic Lamb brought fame and glory to Northamptonshire and England.

Kevin Lyons: All three of them came out of the South African schools coaching programme. I always thought Kirsten would be my type of batsman. Even at seventeen he was strong and aggressive, with a tremendous temperament.

He dearly wanted to join Glamorgan. Not least because he loved rugby. He was a brilliant outside-half and played against the British Lions when he was only eighteen. To have played rugby in Wales would have given him a great thrill. Ironically when he went to Derbyshire he rubbed the salt in a bit by scoring two double centuries against us.

Glamorgan's close link with South Africa was largely responsible for Chris Smith being launched on his meteoric rise into Test cricket, as Kevin Lyons explains:

Our Alan Jones was coaching in Durban and he rated Chris so highly that he encouraged him to think about playing in England.

A few years later Alan was actually going out to bat when Chris popped up at Swansea. He had flown over especially to see if Glamorgan could give him a chance.

He was told that if he proved himself in the South Wales League, he would be given a few games in our second team, but only when Welsh lads were not available.

We had nets at Swansea in those days and they were situated close to where the rugby posts stood in winter. The ground was rough and the ball flew in all directions, but Chris still looked a fine player. He opened the innings for a village club called Gorseinon and came in for a few second-team games when we had a vacancy. I remember discussing with him in earnest the need to be mean. Not to give his wicket away.

Then a great build-up of luck played an incredible part in his breaking through into the big time. Our second team was due to play Hampshire at Bournemouth, and two days before the match I had to apologise to Chris for not having a place for him. As usual he took it well. He understood that we wanted to give our young Welsh players every opportunity to show what they could do.

Next morning his luck started to turn. I was told that one of our first-team players was injured and that a replacement had to come from the seconds. Having organised that I then went back to Chris and told him we now had a place for him in the seconds, provided he still wanted to play. He leapt at the chance and scored a magnificent century.

Though everyone at Glamorgan appreciated his talents we already had our full quota of overseas players so we had no alternative but to let him go at the end of the season.

West Indian pair Richie Richardson and Jeffrey Dujon also escaped the Glamorgan net. Both showed their talents in the South Wales League. Dujon for Swansea and Richardson for Neath. Kevin Lyons says:

We've taken on so many players from other counties and signed so many overseas people that it's not surprising we've been called Dad's Army and the United Nations. If a county side is to engage an overseas player, then he must make the difference between them finishing in the top three and being an average side. Any lower, and they have wasted their money.

At that point with Glamorgan it looked as though Chris Smith's luck had run out, but there was more to come. Hampshire chief coach Peter Sainsbury remembers very clearly that second eleven match at Bournemouth in which Smith played as a late replacement. Sainsbury now takes up the story:

That was the first time I saw Chris. He opened for Glamorgan and murdered us. We had a strong attack, including three from the first team, but he destroyed them all. It was a terrific hundred.

At the end of that season we had to start thinking of who could stand in for Gordon Greenidge, who was needed for a West Indian tour the following summer.

I told our committee of Chris Smith and I praised him as a batsman with world-class potential. They listened to what I had to say and offered him a contract. Then he came into the first team and hit big score after big score. Everyone was impressed.

In fact he had been with us a few months when he came up to me one evening and said he would like to clear his conscience. I had no idea what he meant. He began by asking if I could remember the hundred he hit at Bournemouth. I told him it would always stick in my mind.

So he said, 'Well, I've a confession to make. In the very first over of that match I got an edge, the wicketkeeper caught the ball, but no one appealed. So I stayed and cracked on.'

Extraordinary luck of that sort is probably more important in cricket than in any other sport. A batsman is usually permitted just one mistake. No more. If Chris had been dismissed in that first over we wouldn't have given him a thought. He would probably be back in South Africa now, completely forgotten about.

Instead he is a naturalised Englishman and a front-line

156

batsman. He has a wonderful temperament and is a real workaholic. He is mad about practice. His brother Robin is the same.

Often when I come to the ground at nine o'clock they are both already in the nets. They deliberately come at dawn to be sure no one else gets there first. That's the way they grew up in South Africa. They would be out in the garden at sunrise. At seven o'clock, when their parents were still in bed. The family had a house-servant, and Chris and Robin would tumble him out of bed and make him throw cricket balls at them before they sat down for breakfast.

Always ready to praise good players, Sainsbury is in no doubt that Robin Smith was the best seventeen-year-old batsman he had ever seen.

Robin is extremely strong, particularly on the off-side. And he has a great ability to concentrate for long periods. He scored two hundred for our second team one day and batted five hours. He was oblivious to everyone and everything. An earthquake wouldn't have shifted him. He is obsessed with getting his head down and scoring runs.

Of course, Hampshire's eye for a talented overseas player has never been confined to outstanding batsmen. It seems that whenever they run short of a good quick bowler all they need do is lift the receiver and dial Barbados. Andy Roberts, Malcolm Marshall, Eldis Reifer and Winston Small have all been contacted on the Caribbean hot line.

Careful not to identify their astute Barbados connection, Peter Sainsbury says:

He's a very important man out there. He's also a very good friend of our chairman Charles Knott. All Mr Knott has to do is pick up the telephone and tell him what he wants, and the man will say, 'I think you should try so-and-so.'

We should have signed Winston Small, but the West Indians wanted him. Then our man came up with Eldis. He had never played first-class cricket before. Our man went purely on potential and Eldis proved him right with a bagful of wickets in his first season.

Just as Hampshire have always welcomed world-class players from South Africa, so have their keen South Coast rivals, Sussex.

Garth Le Roux and Kepler Wessels were specially registered to bolster a strong home-bred squad, along with further overseas stars in Imran Khan and Javed Miandad. Stewart Storey says of Wessels:

That man has amazing powers of concentration. If I told him to stay at the crease for two days he would do just that. He thrives on batting every day.

Kepler is a great boundary hitter. One of the best batsmen in the world against a bad ball.

Socially, I'm afraid he had his shortcomings with us. He was a poor mixer. If we were batting he would usually sit in his car and read a book all day. He was a complete loner.

His game went to pieces when he left us to play in Australia. I watched him open against England and his stance was diabolical. When he batted for us he tended to play around his legs which blocked the line of the bat, but he was never as bad as that time against England.

Most quickies in Australia like to bowl short and to their slips. That suits Kepler. He loves to lean back and square cut. Then the England bowlers arrived and found him out. They attacked his leg stump and exposed his weakness. His technique had definitely gone back.

Kepler was with us at the same time as Miandad. In fact, we had four overseas players then, which was ridiculous. Something had to be sorted out. We had to decide which of them was going to win matches for us. Would it be Miandad or Wessels? Which of them in day-to-day cricket would score the most runs?

Miandad was a law unto himself. A poor communicator by any standards. He could hardly speak one word of English when he first arrived. How he ever copes in Wales with Glamorgan is impossible to imagine.

Having released Miandad we then had to decide between Wessels and Le Roux. We all agreed that bowlers win matches, so Wessels left and Le Roux was retained to spearhead our attack with Imran.

In spite of his county's past enthusiasm to engage overseas players Storey makes it plain where he stands on this thorny subject:

When overseas players first came into our game, a rule should have been made there and then to limit each county to one player and to insist that that player was of a proven Test match standard.

Counties who have brought over young, inexperienced players have done extreme damage to our game. Alvin Kallicharran was only seventeen and unheard of when he joined Warwickshire. And now Worcestershire and Hampshire have just signed unknown West Indian teenagers.

Over the years English cricket has produced a Test side for Pakistan and the West Indies. And at the same time our English team has gone hurtling downhill.

Look at Gloucestershire. They had three overseas players, Sadiq, Zaheer and Procter in the first five in the order to the detriment of young Gloucestershire batsmen, offering them no opportunity of first-class cricket.

Having one overseas player was a shot-in-the-arm for many counties, but the whole basic idea has been badly abused.

Once Imran or Le Roux leaves us I hope we shall remain with just one overseas player. For one thing we can't afford any more. Who can?

Far from improving the skills and confidence of our young English cricketers, I believe the army of overseas players have often destroyed good homegrown talent. A player like our David Standing could so easily be overawed when out in the middle with a world-class overseas batsman. Phil Slocombe, of Somerset, comes to mind as another example. When he's at the crease with Viv Richards, he must know the crowd is not there to see him. So what does he do? He pushes for a single to give Richards the strike and snicks a catch and is out. Or he might see Richards wallop a ball over the boundary – then he thinks, 'I could never do that', and loses heart.

If the truth were known, I don't believe any county has truly benefited from having an overseas player. When Viv Richards is dismissed, the Somerset supporters let out a big groan.

Somerset are not alone in the way they treat their young players. Too many talented youngsters are missing out on valuable experience. Counties are reluctant to place responsibility on young shoulders, preferring instead to rely on their star players to score the runs and take the wickets.

Overseas players have also caused problems off the field, not least where money is concerned. The difference in salaries has been so big that bad feeling was bound to come in among other members of the team.

All these factors add up to undermine the confidence of a young professional.

What's more, I don't believe that even someone as good as Imran Khan has had a noticeable effect on our gate. Supporters down here like to admire their own kind. Those born and bred in Sussex.

In the words of chief coach Doug Padgett, sticking rigidly to homegrown players has 'backfired badly' on Yorkshire in recent years.

The influence of overseas stars on other counties has made sure the white rose has not blossomed in the championship since way back in 1968.

In particular, Padgett dreams of finding an all-rounder with the match-winning skills of a Richard Hadlee:

We pride ourselves on being loyal to Yorkshire-born players, though I must be honest and admit that it has backfired on us in recent times.

With one world-class player, say Richard Hadlee, who can bat and bowl at the very top level, we would have been a different force. A man of his class would have made a vast difference to us.

Because of our policy we shall always find ourselves struggling a bit. Even if we had one or two regular Test players, that would also backfire on us. They would miss half our matches, playing for England. That's why the other counties do so well. They lose an overseas player just once in four years. I'd love a player like Richard Hadlee, but I wouldn't go outside Yorkshire for him.

Now that the TCCB are tightening the laws concerning the number of overseas players allowed to each county, I think things will begin to even themselves out and Yorkshire will benefit.

Without being conceited, I know there are people in every county who are envious of our policy. They are just waiting for us to win the championship to prove that it can be done without going outside for players. To some extent we showed what we can do when winning the Sunday League in 1983, though we had a terrible time in the championship.

Unlike other county coaches, I can say that I have produced virtually every player in this club and that gives me tremendous satisfaction. My finger is constantly on the conveyor-belt. If we need a certain type of bowler I can't rush off to Jamaica or Johannesburg with a chequebook and solve the problem overnight. We have to find around twenty-one players, and they all must come from Yorkshire, which is a tall order year after year.

The question of apartheid has divided English cricket, with top players being banned from the England team for their links with South Africa.

The anomalies caused by cricket's stubborn political stand against apartheid could never be better exposed than at Northampton, where their English-born batsman Wayne Larkins is banned from playing Test cricket because he toured in South Africa in 1982, yet his county colleague Allan Lamb, born in Cape Province, is a regular member of the England team.

Larkins was banned for three years, along with such fine English players as Graham Gooch, John Emburey and Derek Underwood.

Northamptonshire's outspoken chief coach Brian Reynolds has firm views on the subject:

They got what they deserved. All of them. They had posed a serious threat to the game as we know it. If what they did had gone unchecked, any number of cricketers would have been put out of a job, myself included.

Having said that, I can understand why they went. It gave them financial security for life. If the offer had come my way I would probably have thought about it, too.

Wayne Larkins is a tremendously aggressive batsman. Just the type England needs. I remember watching him as a young player in the nets. He struck the ball extremely hard. And I shall never forget the way, later on, that he bludgeoned the ball against Yorkshire at Scarborough. He had scored ninety, but there was no careful approach to his hundred. He still kept hammering the ball into the pavilion and over the wall.

My biggest disappointment with Wayne is that he doesn't work hard at his bowling. He can swing the ball both ways, but he doesn't treat his bowling seriously.

Being such a small county, Northamptonshire are forced to cast their net wide to recruit quality players. In recent years Lamb and Rupert Hanley have come in from South Africa, Mushtaq and Sarfraz from Pakistan, Bedi and Kapil Dev from India, and all except three of the 1983 side were anything but Northamptonshire-born.

Without this formidable outside support, Northamptonshire would find it impossible to compete, though Brian Reynolds makes it plain that he is totally opposed to overseas players swamping English cricket:

I don't believe for one minute that any overseas player has brought in more people to watch cricket. What they have done is earn big money. They have taken more out of the game than they have put into it. On that point there can be no argument.

Allan Lamb came to England with Peter Kirsten and Garth Le Roux. They based themselves in Derbyshire and then shopped around for a county. We gave all three a trial in our second team against Yorkshire. We thought it would be a good test for them. Kirsten didn't score many, but Lamb tore them apart. He scored eighty in no time. Richard Lumb skippered the Yorkshire side and he didn't know where to place his fielders. In the end it was a toss-up between Lamb and Kirsten, and our committee went for Lamb.

Leicestershire's Ken Higgs is not at all happy about the ease with which players can switch nationalities:

South African-born cricketers like Lamb, Chris Smith and the others may say they are English – or, in Kepler Wessels' case, Australian. But with no disrespect to them, I think they are just looking for a loophole to play Test cricket. If the rules let them in, they leap at the chance.

I don't blame people like Lamb and Smith for playing for England, but when I see someone like Tony Greig, who captained our country, saying he is South African, I become very angry. The question is, do these players want to live in England twelve months of the year?

Allan Lamb, for example, is a great fellow. I have no grumbles with him. But if there was no England tour, where would he be in winter. In England or South Africa? Are they English or are they not English? If they were born here, then they are English. If they were not, then they don't qualify. That's how I see it.

Would English lads be allowed to play for South Africa or the West Indies? Would they bend the rules for our chaps?

I know nothing about politics. I don't want to know. All I do know is that we are being deprived of seeing a fine South African side in international cricket.

Chris Smith's brother Robin is also available for England now. There seems no end to it. If they are not careful England will finish up with a team of South Africans and West Indians.

Evidently Higgs is far from alone with these fears. The Test and County Cricket Board finally made a positive move in August 1984 to make it harder for South African-born players to represent England.

They proposed that one year should be added to the present four-year residential qualification period for each season of first-class cricket the qualifier had played in his country of origin; that during the qualification period, the player must spend at least 210 nights a year in Britain; and that the qualifier must register as an overseas player in his country of origin.

Leicestershire have indulged in their own spot of overseas recruitment from time to time, though never to the extent of so many other counties.

When Andy Roberts was no longer required by Hampshire, the alert Leicestershire secretary Mike Turner swept into action and the brilliant West Indian bowler justified every vestige of confidence that was placed in him. Ken Higgs has nothing but praise for Roberts:

I had admired Andy right from the start. When he first went to Hampshire he concentrated on bowling the ball as fast as he could from one end of the wicket to the other. Then he noticed that the ball would move off the seam, so he became hungry to know how it was done.

All Andy's bowling was learnt in England. He was a great

worker. It was nothing to see him enter a net at nine in the morning and bowl flat out for an hour or more.

Not everyone works like that. A lot think they don't need nets because they can do well in the middle. But it doesn't always work out that way, as many find to their cost.

Though gushing in his praise of Roberts, a forthright Higgs leaves no one in doubt about his views on overseas players earning their living in English cricket:

When they first came in I thought they were good for the game. Now, I think we could survive without them. The truth is, we educate them. Then they come back with their country and knock hell out of us. In particular, we teach them how to play the moving ball.

The more I look at our local cricket for quick bowlers, the more I realise how badly off this country is. In the West Indies every lad dearly wants to be a fast bowler. When I went there with England, I remember Geoff Boycott going out for a second net after the team had returned to the dressing-room, and he called up fifteen to twenty lads to bowl to him. I watched them closely. They all bowled quickly, but not one of them wore anything on his feet. I remember Geoff saying to them, 'Have you noticed, your feet are bleeding?'

And they smiled back at him and said, 'Oh, don't worry, man, that's just my drag.'

No matter where we went in the West Indies, we saw lads playing cricket. One day we went up into the mountains, drove round a corner and found four lads playing a 'Test match' in the middle of the road. As we approached, they picked up their tin wicket, waited for us to pass, and then put it back and went on playing. We thought it was terrific.

There was a time when just about every lad in England wanted to play cricket and nothing else. Now they have any number of other sports to choose from. The dedication has gone.

Unlike many other counties Surrey, in particular, have not shown any enthusiasm recently to dig deep and sign overseas players.

New Zealand batsman Geoff Howarth joined the county as far back as 1971 while their West Indian paceman Sylvester Clarke came in 1979. Otherwise they have relied on finding talent nearer home, although David Gibson is quick to emphasise that this is not as easy as it sounds. Gibson reckons that scouring the county for talented youngsters has put ten years on his life:

It's hard work. Too many batsmen won't graft. If things don't go right in the first hour, they lose heart. Alec Stewart is an exception, but then his father, Micky, has obviously been a great influence on him. Alec will succeed because he works hard. If we had eleven people with Alec's talent and dedication, we wouldn't need overseas players.

There is little point in spending money to bring on your own young players if, when they reach a position to challenge for a first-team place, you then decide to bring in an overseas player. That's stupid and wasteful. As I see it, the only advantage in having West Indian bowlers in this country is that England batsmen can have valuable experience in playing against them at county level.

Counties are also suffering because very few good players are now coming out of the universities, which has made them think more of bringing in these overseas people.

Surprise, surprise . . . it is now revealed that Nottinghamshire have Leicestershire's magnanimous secretary Mike Turner to thank for bringing the world's leading all-rounder Richard Hadlee to their notice.

Philip Carling, then chief executive at Nottingham, took the call from Turner, who said Hadlee was looking for a job and Leicestershire couldn't take him.

Carling, who later moved to Glamorgan, immediately rang Ken Taylor, then chairman of the cricket committee, and told him of Turner's tip-off.

Being a cautious man, Taylor insisted that before any move was made a swift and confidential check should be made on Hadlee to satisfy everyone that he was a man who could behave himself. Boozers and womanisers were not wanted on any account, no matter how well they played in the middle.

Of course, his background was so good that I didn't think for one moment he was a bit like that, but I still wanted him vetted. And then to sign him at all costs. Philip did the job superbly.

To make room for Richard poor Dilip Doshi, the little

left-armer had to go, but he wasn't really in love with county cricket. He didn't like fielding, batting or exercising. He was a nice chap and a fine bowler, though when he played for us on a sticky wicket he still tossed the ball up. I remember Miandad murdering him in a match we should have won.

Richard Hadlee is a remarkable man. He gave so much in one match against Lancashire that he was too exhausted to walk up the steps. He gets very emotionally involved. The great thing about Richard is that he bowls right on the spot from the word go. Yet all these young chaps say they need time to loosen up and get their length. What rubbish.

If a young player has a technical problem we encourage him to speak to people like Clive Rice and Richard Hadlee. More is learned from speaking to senior players of this calibre than can ever be gained from going in the nets.

Clive is a fine leader. He came here in 1975 when we desperately needed an overseas player to give us impetus. Jackie Bond was with us then and he mentioned Eddie Barlow at first, but I thought Eddie was a bit too old for what I had in mind. We needed a younger man who could spend several years with us.

It was then that Jackie came up with Clive Rice. He had seen him do well with Ramsbottom in the Lancashire League. I was so keen to have him I went straight down to Eastbourne where he was playing in a charity match and signed him without even seeing him play.

I backed my judgement of him as a fellow. He's very straight. Very intelligent. To be honest, he's not a terrific tactician, but he leads by example. I like the way he aims high.

The legendary Gary Sobers set the best possible example to any county cricketer when Nottinghamshire became one of the first English clubs to engage an overseas player in the new wave of foreign recruitment.

At the time everyone agreed it was an inspired move that brilliantly revived a game that was tottering on its last legs.

As we have seen, the presence of an overseas player is not unanimously accepted as good for the game now. Many leading officials, sympathetic to backing Britain, are even hostile to the idea.

So where does Ken Taylor stand, bearing in mind that Nottinghamshire's current strength lies with South African Rice and New Zealander Hadlee?

I find it difficult to argue the point logically. I would hate to lose our two. It's not just because they are tremendous players but it's their whole attitude to the game. They set such a fine example to everyone around them.

Yes, they are expensive, but I consider every penny we pay them is fully earned and fully justified. They are great crowd-pullers.

It's a difficult case to defend because some people say that if we didn't have them we would have more room for local players. I am not sure that would raise the standard, and I can't agree that local lads are suffering at all. If anything, I think they have profited from the presence of Rice and Hadlee.

When Gary came here the game needed a boost. It was awful. It was being ruined by an over-professionalised attitude and a total lack of concern for the spectator. For everyone. I was a committee member at the time, and I shall always remember Gary bowling against Warwickshire. The great Rohan Kanhai was batting and to see them both in combat like that lifted the whole standard of the game. It was truly tremendous.

Derbyshire showed initiative and imagination in completing the most original modern-day signing, when Ole 'Stan' Mortenson became the first Dane to play English championship cricket. Signed in 1983, he bowled 518 overs for 66 wickets to make an immediate impact with his fast-medium deliveries.

Explaining how Derbyshire collared the great Dane, the astute Derbyshire coach Phil Russell says:

It was Ian Buxton who first saw Stan on one of his Scandinavian coaching trips. Then Stan stayed with Ian over here on holiday and Ian asked us if he could bring him along to the nets. We said, 'Yes, please.' We were badly short of bowlers.

I was batting at the time and his first ball whistled past my nose. So I told Tony Borrington to hurry up and put his pads on.

Stan played a few matches in our second team and I told him that if he ever thought of playing in England to contact me.

Two seasons went by and then I heard that Durham had seen him in Denmark and got him qualified as an 'honorary Englishman' through the Common Market laws, though he had not played for Durham because of some domestic problem.

We were desperately short of fast bowlers, so I wrote to him and invited him to play for us, stressing that he would be classed as 'English', of course.

After a week's trial, in which he impressed us a lot, I talked the committee into signing him and he has more than justified my confidence. He's not lightning quick, but he's quick enough. And he's strong and very aggressive. And he bowls straight.

Though enormously pleased with Mortenson, Russell is not shy to lash out at those counties who import players from all corners of the world.

Money has become all-important. There is a real danger now that the wealthy clubs are going to buy up all the best talent. Look at Glamorgan. They have players from everywhere, but the best team they ever put on the field had ten Welshmen in it.

And players are swapping counties at a terrific pace. It is something no one can stop. Once sponsors came into the game, the need to be successful trebled overnight. That's why the overseas player has become so important. I would limit every county to one, though we have two here in John Wright and Michael Holding.

Signing Holding proved a great psychological boost all round, even though we had him for only six weeks of the 1983 season. He definitely helped the morale of our batsmen. Just the thought of knowing he was with us, and not our opponents, did our chaps a power of good. West Indian bowlers seem to have something special in their hearts. They want to bowl fast. And they are tremendous athletes.

John Wright came to us in 1977 after being recommended by Brian Luckhurst. He had played for Kent Seconds and I saw him score 170 at Folkestone. He looked a fine player, so we signed him. We were lucky, I suppose, because Kent already had two overseas chaps in John Shepherd and Asif Iqbal. John Wright is a good county batsman, especially now that he's learned to relax. If he can improve his mental approach still more, he will do even better.

Iqbal is one of only a few overseas players signed by Kent, who have mainly preferred to encourage their own local stock. The Antiguan Eldine Baptiste is another rare recruit who swept into the West Indian team after just one full season of county cricket.
Colin Page: I first noticed Baptiste when touring with Kent in Antigua. He was about seventeen then, and everything he did appealed to me. I asked him if he'd like to play for Kent and made it plain that I'd have no Dutch Auction.

He said 'I'd love to play for you, and there'll be no auction. Viv Richards has said to me, "If Kent offer you a place, snap it up, in case they change their minds."'

Despite the brilliance of both Iqbal and Baptiste, Page would still rather rely on home-grown talent:
I would retire happily if we could field eleven Kent-born players to win the championship. In fact, eleven English players would do.

I am totally opposed to all these overseas chaps coming into our game. English cricket is turning sour because all the best opportunities are being taken by players from other countries. We are offering them an apprenticeship at the expense of our own lads. It's lunacy. We train them to be Test stars. Then they come back and thrash us in the internationals.

Some counties keep telling me they are going bust, but they still manage to pay out astronomical wages to overseas players. Iqbal came to Kent on the same terms as everyone else. We never pay over the odds.

Yorkshire should be applauded long and hard for the lone stand they have taken against imported players. I admire them immensely.

Fifteen years ago, English cricket might have needed a little overseas injection to pep the game up. Gary Sobers did a great job in that respect. Then some counties went berserk and abused the idea. Overseas players came pouring in, and it soon had the inevitable disastrous effect on our national side.

So much cash has been spent on signing these players that little, if anything, is left in the kitty now to attract good local lads. This short-sighted policy has rebounded on everyone. If England have a poor team, enthusiasm dies through the country, crowds drop off, gate money falls and the counties suffer from a low share-out.

The only way to field a good English side is to find and then coach genuine home-grown talent.

Peter Sainsbury agrees:

Too many of our up-and-coming youngsters have been frozen out. Many of them have given up and vanished through sheer frustration.

Desmond Eager's greatest ambition as Hampshire secretary was to field eleven players who were all born in this county. We reached nine once, but he never saw his dream fulfilled. Desmond was so passionately fond of finding home-grown players that he set up a fund to be used exclusively towards attracting young cricketers from within this area.

Middlesex obviously have no regrets about the signing of Wayne Daniel, yet chief coach Don Bennett insists that one overseas player should be enough for any county – 'though it would be hard to kick the rest out.'

Don Bennett: Wayne Daniel was eighteen when he came to us. He was raw and quick. Gubby Allen and I watched him bowl for the West Indian Young Cricketers at Lord's and decided to sign him, though we knew he was a slight gamble.

Looking back, it was a good day's work. Wayne has been a massive asset. He thinks about the game, and he thinks about other people. He is always asking about players in the second team. He is just as happy bowling to our young lads in the nets as he is thumping the ball down in Test matches.

Wayne has been a credit to himself, to our club and to his country. He's a terrific bloke.

Everyone marvels at the extraordinary way the West Indians continue to produce their tremendous mixture of fast bowlers and attacking batsmen. Don Bennett identifies several factors which help to make this possible:

In Barbados lads play on pitches where the ball skids through. It sharpens the batsmen and gives encouragement to bowlers.

Even more important, the schools pick teams that combine men and boys. Lads of sixteen or seventeen can be asked to face bowlers like Wayne Daniel or Malcolm Marshall while still in the sixth form. It gives them immense experience and allows them to assess their ability at a very young age. Even before they leave school they know what chance they have of making a living from the game.

Of course, there is not much work to go around. Cricket is a way out for them, like football in Brazil, and the way boxing used to be in Britain.

In Antigua the young ones usually learn their cricket by imitation. Everyone wants to be a Viv Richards or an Andy Roberts.

And the weather is so fantastic. They can play cricket all the year round.

John Savage agrees with Don Bennett that every county should be limited to one overseas player and he adds emphatically:

Local lads must not be left out in order to accommodate people from all over the world.

In the case of Clive Lloyd I think our young players have looked up to him and reaped the benefit of playing alongside such a fine sportsman.

Like everyone else we are always on the look-out for good fast bowlers. At one time we had Colin Croft and Michael Holding, though neither of them achieved what I thought they would.

Croft was quick in his first season, but very raw. He disappointed me. With his pace I thought we had someone who could fire back, but it never happened.

In some cases the West Indian bowlers can't cope with seven-day cricket. It's a big change from what they've been used to back home. Out there they don't play every day. They don't rush up and down motorways. To some extent they can take it easy.

8

Life at Lord's with the Godfather

Chief coach at the superb Lord's indoor school for the past eight years, the thoughtful Don Wilson is still showing the same qualities of imagination and inventiveness that made him such a formidable bowler. The former Yorkshire and England left-arm spinner has now come up with a revolutionary idea for preventing English county cricket from being overrun by overseas players:

As a typical Yorkshireman I think there are enough good cricketers in this country. The first-class game should be left to them.

If we must have overseas players – and I don't want them – I think an eighteenth 'county' should be created for them alone. In this way they could play each county twice and continue to entertain the public without depriving all our fine young players of the chance to prove themselves.

Some years ago there was a saying, 'A good Yorkshire side means a good English side.' And if someone didn't quite make it with Yorkshire, he joined another county, like an overseas player. Jim Laker was just one.

Year after year we have several brilliant players at Lord's who are looking for a future in the game. But overseas players are keeping them out. Counties are preferring to buy success, which I think is a disgrace. They keep bringing in these West Indian eighteen-year-olds because they think they can get some mileage out of them.

Eldine Baptiste is a good example. He's been with Kent for years. They gambled on him being a good player and he's now in the Test team. I know it sounds fabulous. But why didn't Kent put an English lad in there?

In his seven years at Lord's the avuncular Wilson has played Godfather to around two hundred aspiring lads and has supplied as many as thirty-three to the first-class game. The terrible irony is that of the four who have so far played for their country only one, Norman Cowans, is English. The others are New Zealanders Martin Crowe and Gary Robertson, and Australian Wayne Phillips. Wilson says of Crowe:

He was with me a year. He looked a class player, though I did tighten him up a lot. Oh, yes, there is plenty you can teach them. When Martin came he was a terrible big-shot player. So I had to steady him down. I had to teach him how to play the good ball.

I had to tell him to say 'Right, when I score fifty, I'm going to get eighty, and then a hundred, and then a hundred and fifty.'

That's self-discipline. I didn't tell him, 'This is how you play the cover-drive. Or this is how you hook.' I didn't do that. I showed him what top cricket requires.

Martin came here under an arrangement we have with the New Zealand Cricket Board of Control. They send over a young prospect every year. Martin was just seventeen years of age, and almost as soon as he arrived he played for the Lord's groundstaff against the MCC. Colin Cowdrey captained the MCC and he set us 215 to win in very little time. Then this lad Crowe went to the wicket and cracked a fabulous hundred off a strong attack that included Tim Lamb and Mushtaq Mohammad.

Towards the close we needed four to win and Crowe needed six for his hundred. And he stepped outside his leg stump and thumped the ball into the Tavern Stand.

What impressed me most about Martin was that he always wanted to beat you. We spent hours and hours in the nets together. He was incredibly dedicated. If he had a weakness, it was on his leg stump. So every time we went to the nets we had a bet. I set an imaginary field and if he hit the ball in the air towards a 'fielder', it cost him a pound. And if he stayed in twenty minutes without being out, he got one from me. He was good. He was determined not to get out. He cost me a fortune.

In those days he tended to sweep a lot. I wanted him to play straight. So he concentrated on hitting the ball through mid-wicket and mid-on. This part of his game improved enormously. He's very strong in that area now.

Then I took him up to Bradford in the Yorkshire League. That is the hardest grounding a player can have. I put immense pressure on him. So he had to become a better player. And he did. He broke every League record. He scored more fifties, more hundreds and more runs than anyone before him. Then he went into the Lancashire League, which put even more pressure on him because he had to bat and bowl.

He went back to New Zealand a mature player, and I was not surprised by his magnificent performances against England, especially his brilliant maiden Test century.

But how can anyone explain why he went to Somerset for just one season while Richards and Garner were with the West Indians? If he wanted county cricket, I thought he should have stayed much longer. That was buying a ready-made player – buying success. It's beyond me, and I'm sad about it. There are enough English lads around who would have loved the chance. That's where the counties are going wrong.

It was a great thrill for me while watching New Zealand and England on television to see Gary Robertson bowling to Norman Cowans, and Martin Crowe fielding the ball. All three had been with me at Lord's.

And Wayne Phillips?

He came here on a scholarship as one of Australia's promising cricketers. He was supposed to stay three months, but he liked it so much that he stayed six. He lived at my house and the lads nicknamed him 'Ripper'.

The night before he left we held a party and presented him with a memento to remember his time with us. When I woke next morning I found a £5 note taped to the mirror in my lounge. There was also a note with it which said, 'The first time I play for Australia, buy yourself a drink out of this.' And he signed it 'Ripper'.

To be honest, I never thought he would ever play for his country. They had so many good players pressing for the few batting places. Then he was involved in a magnificent stand of 250 for New South Wales. He rang me that night from his home to tell me about the innings, and said that I would be spending the £5 very soon.

Even then, I didn't think it possible. Of course, a few weeks later I was proved wrong. Wayne was picked for Australia's tour of India and he opened the batting. On the night he was selected, he telephoned me again and said I could now go into London and have a meal on his fiver. But I never did. I decided to keep it. One day I shall frame it. It means a lot to me now.

When he first came to me, Wayne wanted to hit every ball out of sight. He was extremely aggressive. And just as I did with Martin, I tightened him up. I taught him to select the right ball.

Damian d'Oliveira, Norman Cowans, Asif Din, Neil Williams, Paul Smith and Dermot Reeve are just some of the fine players Wilson has sent out to the counties. Of the young d'Oliveira, he says:

Like one or two others, Damian thought he was something of a superstar when he started. Then he had to work. Being on the groundstaff is a great leveller.

If lads think they are special, we have to bowl them out. That's what brings them down. When they've had a bad day, or a bad week, or a bad second team game, I usually say, 'Well, it seems you're not quite as good as you thought you were.' And that's it. They are ticked off. And I expect them to do something about it. If I'm very cross, I tell them I don't need them the following month, though I do. It puts pressure on them. It makes them think. All of a sudden, players like Damian will realise that life is slipping away. That they need to be careful.

When Damian left here he had become a tremendous character, and he's gone back to Worcester and done a wonderful job. I am full of praise for his father. Before Damian came here, Basil rang me one morning and said, 'Don, should I give up being the coach at Worcester and let my lad have a chance here?'

Now for someone to say that must have taken a lot of courage. I told Basil to stay where he was and to send Damian to me.

Yet for every five outstanding successes at Lord's there is always one major disappointment to remind the over-confident that even the most talented can fail when the vital test is applied. Raymond Berry is a first-class example. Hailed by Wilson as a player to behold, he left Lord's for his home county, Lancashire, and has ended up in his father's furniture business.

Don Wilson: Raymond Berry is a talented player. I thought a lot of him. I'm afraid he's just missed out. But he's only twenty, so time is on his side. He has played for Blackpool and is now trying to become a county player by scoring a lot of runs in the League.

Raymond was a terribly nervous lad. It was his only failing. He even showed it in the nets. He would say, 'I've got the shakes', which no one should ever admit. We all get very nervous. We all have butterflies. But we don't all talk about it. We don't spread it around. I'm afraid Raymond did, and people took advantage of it.

I made him headboy over all the groundstaff, hoping the position would give him confidence, but he couldn't handle it.

Yet, all is not lost. With his talent he could still become a big name in county cricket.

I have reminded Raymond that Jack Simmons made it at Blackpool. I told him, 'You are very lucky to have your father's business to fall back on. You have a job, so the pressure is off. Once you start to play the way you can, you won't have to worry about whether you will score forty or a hundred.'

Raymond had a phenomenal record on our staff. For him not to be playing county cricket is unreal.

Dealing with a player like Raymond, you need to be a psychologist as well as a coach. And I am a big psychologist. Attitude of mind is a major part of the game.

When I went to South Africa, I met players like Eddie Barlow and the Pollock brothers. Imagine coaching players like them. Graeme Pollock was a fine player, but he wanted to retire. He kept saying 'I can't get a run. I must wear glasses.' So I worked at him. I got him to want to play. And he had his best season. Not only that, his team won the Gillette Cup and they'd never won anything before. So their chairman came to me and said, 'How the hell did you do that?'

For once they believed in themselves. Graeme got his appetite back. I reminded them that cricket is a thinking game. Can you imagine me having to tell the great Graeme Pollock he is a good player? I also had to get them to believe in Kenny McEwan who, I think, is a first-class player. They didn't rate him over there.

Unlike most senior coaches, Wilson opposes rather than approves the wearing of helmets, both by batsmen and close-in fielders:

The helmet has helped to take a lot of glamour out of the game. Catches are going to places now that they never went to before.

All of a sudden, deep fine-leg and deep square-leg are wicket-taking positions. If a bowler rattles the ball around a batsman's head that's where he's going to hit it.

In my time the ball was pitched up and there were three slips and a couple of gullys. That was when we saw all the marvellous shots through extra-cover. There was only one man deep on the off-side, and just a mid-wicket on the leg side.

Peter May and I have discussed this many times. It was a thrill to see his mid-wicket shot for four, and Cowdrey's cover-drive, and Graveney's marvellous elegance. They were the days when the crowd went home remembering classic shots.

Now there is so much short bowling, we no longer see those shots. It's all hooking and pulling. And I blame the helmet. It has allowed the quick bowler to say, 'I can bowl short all the time.' And the batsmen have said 'Right, if you bowl short, I know where I'm going to crack you.'

Cricket has lost some of its art.

If bowlers pitched the ball up, helmet manufacturers would be out of business.

Obviously there are far more fast bowlers in county cricket now and Test matches are dominated by them. Batting against the West Indians must be horrifying.

They are no quicker now than they were thirty years ago. Michael Holding is no faster than Wes Hall. But in my day they went in pairs: the West Indians had Hall and Griffith, and England matched them with Trueman and Statham. And every side had two good spinners and a medium-pacer. Now a batsman has to go in and face four quickies in a row. And it doesn't last for ninety minutes or so. It can continue all day, with no respite.

The balance of the game has altered dramatically. It is for that reason alone, I think, that the helmet has come in.

I remember a lad from Essex being hit, and the ball just about stuck in his teeth. It was a horrible sight. With a helmet on, the ball would have struck his visor and gone away.

The great Kanhai was also hit, playing against Yorkshire. He was an avid hooker, and every time he hooked, he put so much effort into his shot he lost his balance and fell over.

This day he laid into Fred Trueman at Leeds with a massive pull shot and the ball went for six. Fred was furious. Next ball he ran up and slammed one down and Kanhai was nowhere near it. The ball screamed through, nicked his ear and took a piece of the lobe with it. Now that was too close for comfort.

Yet even in those circumstances I would still prefer not to see the helmet. I feel it gives those batsmen who are not quite good enough a better chance and more confidence. There's something false about it all.

Close-in fielders should also be made to do without helmets. The principle is unfair. All right, I suppose Brian Close invented that silly position. He did marvellously well there for Ray Illingworth and me. He picked up thirty to forty wickets a season for me in that bat-pad area, just in front.

But he was fearless. He took some terrible knocks, but he never winced. That was courage. I never felt he was shell-shocked. I never felt his nerve was going. He was rock firm. We all knew that if Brian was hit on the head he was a better player.

His batting was the same. I remember we played Derbyshire on the most dreadful wicket at Leeds and needed ninety to win when Brian went in. Harold Rhodes was bowling at his quickest and his first ball hit Brian smack on the head. And we all said in the dressing-room, 'That's it. They'll never get him out now.' He deliberately took Harold on, scored 45 and we won the match. He was unreal.

Brian was a curious fellow. If the ball hit him on the toe, he was carried off. That's what he was like. Injury and pain didn't exist. He would say to me, 'It doesn't hurt, you know.' He was probably hit on the body more than any other player in the game, but I never once heard him say, 'My goodness, my ribs hurt.' I couldn't believe it, because there were times when I knew I'd be in absolute agony. But that's the way he played the game. He loved to say it didn't hurt.

His courage was colossal. How can any cricket follower forget the day he took that physical battering from the West Indians at Lord's? Hall and Griffith left him black and blue. He came back to Yorkshire after that match with 32 bruises on his body and he paraded around in the nude for us all to count them. He loved it.

No, I never saw his courage wane. Not even fielding close. He even asked me to bowl the occasional full toss. It takes a very brave man to do that.

Coaching at Lord's caters for all ages from six to sixty, with prodigious attention paid to aspiring teenagers, and Don Wilson loves to recall two instances that involved the sons of famous cricketing fathers:

I am very lucky to have players like John Hampshire to help with the coaching. Then one night he telephoned and asked if he could bring his two lads with him. One was nine and the other ten.

'Of course,' I said. 'They needn't play in your net.'

John had been sad because neither of them had ever played cricket seriously, and they never even spoke to him about the game. And he so much wanted them to be cricketers like himself.

So he brought them down and they had two days here. One of them was a left-arm spinner and the other bowled leg-breaks. They left me on a Saturday afternoon and went straight back to Rotherham. I was sitting down to dinner that evening when the telephone rang. It was John. He had just arrived home and he was so excited he couldn't wait to ring me.

'You have done me one of the greatest favours of my life,' he said. 'Do you know, my lads haven't stopped talking about cricket for two and a half hours up the motorway. I'm nearly in tears here. I'm just ringing to say thanks for giving them the chance.'

One of those lads now plays for Derbyshire Under-15s and

John goes with him whenever he can. But it wouldn't have happened if the lads hadn't come here and tasted cricket for themselves. They caught the bug. That's great.

John is a hard man and a tremendous coach. He knows all about pressure, which can't be said for every mother and father. Parents frighten me. They get so het up. They stand on the balcony here and I see their lads looking up at them.

A lot of boys are pushed to the extreme. I wish parents would say, 'Right, son, just go out and enjoy yourself. How lucky you are to be such a good player.' Of course, lads have to be bowled out. They have to bowl badly. They must expect more bad days than good days. Yet some parents think because a lad gets his stumps knocked over once, that's the end of the world.

I was lucky. My mother and father knew nothing about cricket. My father never bowled a ball in his life. Fathers shouldn't tell sons they have played a silly shot. They should offer a listening ear. A shoulder to cry on. Disappointed lads need encouragement, not a good roasting.

It is my belief that if a lad is in a net for fifteen minutes, he can absorb only six to seven minutes of what he is told. If I spoke to a boy for fifteen minutes non-stop, nothing would stick. And he would be bored. He would keep thinking, 'I'm doing everything wrong', and that would destroy him. No matter what age he is, or what type of person he is, no one likes being told over and over again that he is doing something wrong.

That's why clubs are so good now. In my day, clubs couldn't stand the sight of children. They were a nuisance. Yet practically every club has a junior side now and they can't do enough for the young ones. Clubs have replaced the schools in giving young people a chance to play the game. Only public schools do the job properly now. The average Secondary Modern doesn't have the time or the teachers.

Lads who want to get on in the game come here in droves. Not all of them are magic. Many will be very ordinary players, perhaps in the third team, or even the scorer. But it's a tremendous thrill for me to see them wanting to be involved.

Mike Brearley sets a fine example to all parents when he brings his lad Misha here. Misha was just six when he came here first. He couldn't bat or bowl. He merely wanted to be involved.

Mike is a clever man. He's in the business of psychology. That's why he was such a good captain. Right from the start he never never interfered with Misha's game. Yet he has always noticed when the boy has bowled someone out or played a good shot. He is very proud, though he never says a word on the balcony. He's never pushed, and Misha is a good player now. Mike doesn't say, 'That was an awful shot', because he knows it's the worst thing anyone can do. It's marvellous how he remembers the good bits of Misha's net. That's obviously why he was such a fine captain.

The boy, too, knows he's a Brearley. And he knows that all the other lads know. That can't be easy. I feel sorry for all those sons who have to follow in the footsteps of famous fathers. No one will judge them on their own merits.

Yorkshire had the problem with Richard Hutton. No matter where he went, Richard was always told, 'You will never be as good as your dad.' Or, 'Your dad would never have played that shot.'

But that's a load of old cobblers, because Len did play some bad shots. Not many, I admit, but he did play them from time to time. Everyone does.

Billy Sutcliffe suffered more than anyone. He was a fine player, but when Yorkshire made him captain he couldn't stand the pressure. Everyone picked on him because he was the son of the great Herbert Sutcliffe. It was terrible to live with.

That's why I take my hat off to Mike Brearley. He comes here with his lad, he encourages him, and they must talk about cricket all the way home. That's tremendous.

The current emphasis on physical fitness and all the many methods used to achieve peak condition is a subject on which Don Wilson loves to extemporise:

I shall probably upset one or two county coaches, but I am staggered by what cricketers are asked to do now to get themselves fit. I know they have to be one hundred per cent in heart and limb because it's a seven-day job. But cricketer's shouldn't have to train to run a mile in three minutes.

And all this body-building that's going on. It's like preparing for the Commonwealth Games. In my day all we did was bat and bowl. We played ourselves into shape. If Fred Trueman didn't go on tour he would sink a few drinks and come back carrying a few pounds overweight. So he went into the nets for two hours a day and worked himself into condition. He just bowled and bowled.

I've seen some crazy situations. The weather has been beautiful and players have been chased up and down banks doing Commando training. The nets have not been used. Then when all this donkey work has been done they've staggered down to the nets, and it hasn't stopped raining. So they've ended up without batting.

All this fitness fanaticism came in with the one-day game. It's bad thinking. A professional cricketer must get himself fit, certainly, but also must practise his skills, so that when the season begins he is bowling length and line like clockwork.

But this is not happening. Even Test bowlers are no longer coming in off their normal long run-up, and the number of no-balls they are sending down is alarming. They may be physically fit, but when it comes to producing the skills for which they are paid, they are plain rusty.

With so many people now going abroad to play in winter, they are shattered before the season even starts. A three-week break is the most they can expect. And they spend all that time running up and down the hills. It's terrifying. Players in my day could never have done it.

When August comes they are down on their knees. All that physical nonsense can make the difference between winning and losing a title. Just tilting the balance.

Brushing up on their fielding is also important. I've introduced a new exercise at Lord's. I've had a large white circle painted on a wall. It's eight feet in diameter and I roll a ball out and ask the lads to run in and throw at it. In one session as many as thirty-seven out of forty failed to hit the bull's eye. I was horrified. I called them together and said, 'Do me a favour, find a river and try skimming a pebble across it.'

We were always doing that. And having apple fights. But lads don't do that type of thing now. It's all computers and videos. That's what's changed. Lads are not leaving their rooms any more. So they come here and they can't throw.

To see a lad of sixteen who can't throw a ball is a big worry to someone like me. And I know that when they go back to school, all they'll do is bat, bowl and practise a few high catches. They've lost the art of under-arm flicks and skills of that sort. County players are brilliant at it. They work hard to achieve the highest standards.

Bowlers have all my sympathy these days, up against all those batsmen with the massive bats. A bowler can beat a player through the air, and on the pitch, but the ball will fly over extra-cover. Bowlers no longer get the threequarter edge. Batsmen can mishit and the ball still zooms into the distance. In my day it was a catch. Bowlers used to say that if they got a threequarter bat they had won the contest.

Maybe that's why the spinners have gone from the game. They get hammered now. These bats are devastating. They've transformed the game. It's all crash, bang, wallop. I miss the elegance, the timing, the lovely placing of the ball through a gap for two or three. All that's gone now.

The one-day matches have turned the game upside down. The 55 and 60-over contests provide good cricket, but the 40-over game is just a big slog.

The only good the 40-over game has done is turn up some brilliant fielders. And made captains think harder. They are setting a tighter field. A bowler can sling rubbish down all afternoon now and still end up with nought for 30. He can be thumped to deep square point and concede only one. In a three-day match it would be four and he wouldn't be bowling much longer. The truth is, the 40-over game is keeping mediocre bowlers in business.

Don Wilson is adamant that cricket is crying out for more specialists and that counties are damaging themselves by trying to squeeze every ounce of versatility from players who don't have the overall skills to meet the demands:

Wicketkeepers have it worst. Even Test sides are preferring to pick wicketkeepers who bat a bit rather than have the best wicketkeeper who might not be capable of scoring as many runs. And it's backfiring, because the wicketkeeper–batsman is dropping vital catches, and those are costing matches. For the best balance, a county side should have five specialised batsmen, a good all-rounder, two quickies and two spinners. That's why Middlesex are such a fine side. Players like Gatting, Radley, Edmonds, Emburey and Daniel are all specialists.

To be fair, the game is turning full circle now. The spinner is ready to show his strength again. Nick Cook proved that in 1983. Batsmen have forgotten how to play the ball that is flighted up to them. Even in the one-day game there is panic immediately the ball is thrown up. Batsmen don't know whether to have a whack or play straight.

In the fifties and sixties every side had a bowler like Cook. It hurts me when I look through the sides now and see there are barely five left-armers left in the game. Cook has come to the fore because what he does is basic. He bowls the ball straight and pitches it up. Bedi did the same. He proved the value of a good left-armer.

Considering that Don Wilson was a slow left-armer himself, perhaps it is not surprising that he wishes to promote the importance of this type of bowler.

Six Test matches for England between 1969 and 1972, and eighteen seasons in a powerful Yorkshire side emphasises his immense capability with the ball, so it's only natural that his eyes are constantly scrutinizing the Lord's nets for a young man who can bring back the memories.

One of Wilson's earliest first-class games was against Middlesex at Headingley, a match made truly memorable thanks to the kindness of Denis Compton. Even now, twenty-three years later, a tremor still comes into Wilson's voice as he recalls the occasion:

Alan Moss had bowled me for nought and we were all out for 120. I felt rotten. You think the world's at an end when you've been knocked over for nought.

Middlesex went in, and Jack Robertson and Bill Edrich batted well. I wasn't asked to bowl on the first day. Then, at five minutes past one on the second day, the captain decided to put me on. I looked at the board and saw that Denis Compton was 82 not out.

My first ball to him was a full toss, but instead of hitting it out of sight, he pushed it back to me. Then I dropped a bad one outside his leg stump and he didn't play it at all. It turned out that my first three overs to the great Denis Compton were all maidens.

After lunch the ball was given to Mel Ryan and Fred Trueman. Denis was buzzing. He whacked a few fours but was then out on 98.

I was standing at mid-on, and as he passed me, he said, 'I know you have just come into the game, but if you have as much fun out of cricket as I have, you will have a marvellous life.'

It was only then that I realised he had deliberately pushed the ball back to me. Deliberately let the bad ones go by. And I thought, 'That's one hell of a man.'

Since then the lads have said he could have raced to his hundred off me. But that's how unselfish he was. Fantastic. That wouldn't happen today.

One of the things which worry Wilson deeply about the modern game is the deterioration of the pitches:

The truth is, groundsmen no longer get up at six and sit on the heavy roller all morning. They're in at nine and roll for an hour. That's why the pitches have become so slow. They are made for medium-pacers now.

Places like Headingley and Lord's often suffer from too much cricket. They can be overused. The roots go, from all the wear and tear. Wickets get tired, just like fast bowlers. Pitches were much greener in my day. Much lusher. Trent Bridge was fast and flat. It's hardly that now.

Given his way, Don Wilson would cut back heavily on the international programme. It is not just the pitches, he reckons, but players too who are over-used:

There are too many Test matches now. And the counties, who pay the wages, are losing out. Their star men are away too often.

We seem to be in Australia every winter now. I have always thought that going to a country every four years was best.

Playing cricket is a hard life. Five-day Tests, three-day county matches, and any number of one-day games add up to a strenuous time. That's why the game is losing its momentum.

It's also too defensive now. When I played in county matches we wanted to bowl the opposition out twice. Now we have this peculiar points system. It baffled me for ages.

Bowl tight and we'll be all right, that's the attitude now. You don't need to watch the first two days of a county match any longer. I can turn up at three o'clock on the third day and know precisely what a side will be chasing because the captains have worked out that a hundred runs can be scored in twenty overs. Captains don't go to their bowlers now and say, 'How long will it take you to get this lot out?'

We used to dangle carrots. We used to say, 'Now, you have to score 65 or 70 in an hour.' They were exciting games. But it's all so computerised now. It's like putting a coin in a cigarette machine and seeing the same thing come out time and time again.

As the Godfather at Lord's, the abrasive, likeable Wilson lives in a comfortable house situated behind a tall wall at the Nursery End and little more than a cricket pitch away from his indoor school.

Every year towards the end of April as many as twenty-five lads arrive to join the groundstaff, where they will learn and mature under Wilson's aggressive, yet sympathetic supervision.

Don Wilson: You can imagine what it's like with so many lads seeking their own identity. I have to be tough, or they'd crucify me. And though I want each one of them to be an individual in his own right, I must still mould them into a spirit of friendship so that they are willing to work with one another.

Co-operation is something that has gone out of cricket. People are too selfish now. 'I'm all right, to hell with everyone else' – that's the present-day attitude.

In my time, we made sure we helped each other. We passed tips down the line. Ray Illingworth, for instance, kept a little black book in which he made notes about batsmen who played well on the leg side or the off. And he would read it out to us. No one gives that type of assistance now.

Because of the money in the game, players are determined to keep their places, so the last thing they'll do is pass on information. When a lad leaves me, I like to think that he's learnt the pleasure of helping someone else. That he's learned to socialise.

Many of them have never been to London before, so I encourage them to see the West End, and to take a look at Soho. I consider it part of their education. But it's not nightclubs every night. If that were the drill they'd be finished.

I don't even lay down late-night rules any longer, though at one stage I used to make regular calls at their hostel. I go about twice a year now, usually when they've had a water fight and things have got out of hand.

Whenever a lad has a birthday, I always try to fix up a party for him. Then in the middle of the season, I hold a fancy-dress night. I do it to cheer people up. That's the tricky time when lads may be homesick or fed up with bowling and batting against the same people day in, day out.

But the end-of-season party is the best by far. I put it on in my garden after the NatWest final. Players from both sides always come along and the money collected from the sale of scorecards is put in a kitty for drinks. When it first started, about sixty people turned up. Now we have about 180. Everyone wants to be there.

It's a great night for the lads. They learn to speak to older players, and they learn to serve them drinks. Colin Milburn and Fred Trueman are regulars. And the whole West Indian team came one year.

I encourage lads to bring their parents, so that if fathers and mothers want to talk to me, they have a nice, relaxed atmosphere in which to chat. And I always ask lads to bring their girlfriends. I like to meet them. I like to ask them what they think of their man playing cricket. Because I'm with them for so long, I begin to feel like a parent. I want to know as much as I can about the people who are close to them.

During the evening I stop the party for a minute or two and present an award to the Boy of the Year – not to the lad who has done best on the field, but to the one who has contributed most to the groundstaff.

While the best lads are usually away playing matches, the less fortunate have to stay behind to do pavilion duties, work at the nets, or even score. They are the bread-and-butter boys.

Without them, there would be no groundstaff here. They are the backbone. So it's always one of those lads. Maybe one who is disappointed in himself. The others may be bragging about their averages, so an award like that can give him a lift.

Aggression is another part of the game I try to work on. I'm a bit aggressive myself. I always shout a lot. I let them know it is not an easy world outside. I let them play for as many counties as they can during a season. A county coach may ring up and say 'I'm desperate for a seamer. Can you let me have two lads?' So I push them out. It toughens them up, because the players already in the club don't want them around. Oh, yes, these county players may look nice on the outside, but behind the mask they are usually muttering 'Those MCC groundstaff chaps. What the hell are they doing here?'

Discipline comes high up my list of priorities. Not one of my lads is allowed to go to a match without his blazer and tie. Back in my Yorkshire days, Brian Sellers brought me up that way. That's why I want them to be smart. Anyone who looks sloppy usually plays sloppy. I know they play hell about it, but I won't budge. Some of them have asked to grow a beard, but I won't hear of it.

That's another bit of Brian Sellers coming through in me. He was aggressive. He would call you all the names under the sun and then say, 'Right, I think it's time we went off for a drink.' And the rollicking would be forgotten – at least, by him!

When the lads leave for the counties a lot of what I've instilled will probably be forgotten overnight. That's a pity, because cricket could do with more goodwill. I'm appalled by the cheating that's come into the game. It's out of hand. Batsmen no longer walk when they know they've snicked a catch. And it's disgusting the way players glare and harass umpires. I wouldn't be an umpire if I was offered a fortune.

Umpires in my time were terrific characters. The help I got from Syd Buller and people like Dai Davies, Alec Skelding and Frank Chester was phenomenal. I think that mutual respect has gone. Today everyone seems to be around the bat, throwing up his arms and appealing.

I shall never forget the umpire who stood at Hull in Fred

Trueman's last match against Surrey in 1969. He was fat and jolly. A Yorkshireman. He was on the list for just a year, which was not entirely surprising.

It was getting very late on the last day and we couldn't get Younis Ahmed out. Knowing it was Fred's last appearance there, we took the new ball at five to five, with the match due to end at 5.30.

Fred was shattered. He could hardly walk back to his mark. Then some wag in the crowd shouted out 'Come on, Fred, Yorkshire expects.' And Fred started to cry. Tears rolled down his cheeks.

The only reason we took the new ball was for Illy and me to have something that would bounce a lot higher. Time was rattling by with the quickies on, so Fred came off and Ray went on at one end, and I took over where the fat umpire stood.

Ray dismissed Younis, which meant the tailenders came in. Then I was left to bowl to Robin Jackman, their last man. With just four balls of the last over to go, I ran up and hit him on the pad.

'Howzat!' I yelled.

And the smiling, happy, fat umpire put up his finger and said, 'That's out – and we've won the Championship!'

Surrey were absolutely furious. Whether Jackman was out or not, I don't know, but that umpire was a Yorkshireman through and through. Everyone wanted to get that wicket because it meant so much to us to win the title, but I don't think there was any cheating.

When batsmen don't walk, it puts pressure on umpires. I feel sorry for them. Cheating is quite universal now. Sometimes my lads will walk even if the ball bounces in front of a fielder. That's trying to be too fair, and it annoys me. If a batsman gets a thick nick and it goes to the wicketkeeper, he is out. He knows when he has touched the ball. He should walk.

Just as I'm a stickler for discipline, I feel the same about practice, though some players hate nets and are very bad players in them.

I don't think Botham is a good net player. He just goes in to smack the ball. But Richards treats a net like a Test match. He is a dedicated net player. Perhaps that's why he is such a magnificent batsman. He treats everything as serious business.

Viv batted against me early in his career and he keeps reminding me about it. We had a great contest. I was bowling for the Duchess of Norfolk's Eleven at Arundel, and Viv was in the West Indian side.

I was an old guy then and I bowled him a maiden. He didn't like that. He doesn't like a maiden bowled to him by anyone, let alone by an old man.

And I had reached the fifth ball of the second over and he still hadn't scored off me. I can see him now. As I ran up to bowl, he stepped outside his leg stump and cracked me effortlessly over extra-cover for six. It was one of those fabulous, unforgettable shots. And he winked at me, which was even more degrading.

Next over, I kept him quiet again, so he came down the pitch at me and was stumped.

Later on, we met in the bar and he said, 'I find it damn difficult with you. With the Underwoods and bowlers like him I can play early. Provided I keep my head still the ball comes flat at me. I put my foot down the line of middle-and-off and I play where I want to.

'The problem when playing you is that I have to lift my head up and then down when judging the ball in flight. It's during that split second that I have to decide whether to go down the wicket and attack or push the ball back.'

We all remember the saying, 'He who hesitates is lost.' Well, no one can hesitate in cricket. Everything depends on split-second decisions.

I tell every lad who comes to me that if he can bowl a maiden in his first over he's cracked it. That's very important for a bowler. When he runs up he must keep saying, 'Maiden! Maiden!' It's a great boost.

Viv is a magnificent player, but I wouldn't put him ahead of the other Richards. I rated Barry tremendously highly. They belong to different eras, that's what is so nice about it. One great player following another. Len Hutton was marvellous, but Peter May sticks out above them all. He could do the lot. He clipped it through mid-wicket, played it straight, and always found the gaps.

I bowled to him at the Oval one day and thought I had deceived him with my flight. But he advanced two steps and timed the ball so beautifully that it went high over the stand into the road, and literally rolled down the steps of the tube station.

It was a magnificent shot. Effortless. What made it even worse for me was that I thought I had tricked him. I thought I had him caught at deep mid-off. But the ball kept going higher and higher and farther and farther into the distance. That was very impressive.

The Lord's groundstaff is made up of twenty-five lads who usually include one player from Australia and another from New Zealand.

They arrive in April and stay until September. Over the next three summers they remain together and play virtually all the county second teams, the main public schools, and the MCC staff itself. Wilson's likely lads also sell scorecards, work in scoreboards, pick up litter, put down groundsheets and roll out the covers.

Don Wilson: They come here at eighteen, preferably after they've gained their academic qualifications, because many of them won't make the grade at cricket. Lads of twenty-one and upwards are not much good to me. If they haven't made it by then, there is little hope for them.

In their first summer we basically see if they like it here. Many come in and say, 'My goodness, this is a great holiday, isn't it?' Unfortunately cricket at this level is nothing like a holiday. It's hard work. They can net in the morning, play a match in the afternoon, and still bowl to Members in the evening.

By August, many of them have had enough. They want to be out. It's not the life for them. After a year I can usually tell a lad what chance he has of making the grade.

If he's not a Londoner, coming to the big city can be a tremendous change from life back home. All my lads live together in a hostel at Hampstead. Breakfast and dinner are provided at the hostel, and whenever the lads are playing away their evening meal is always paid for. The wages are not particularly high, but it's a start. Some earn £50 a week, and in their last year with us it goes up to £80, which I think is good for someone doing his apprenticeship.

Being at Lord's is a bit of a shop window. Counties will ring me in mid-season and ask if I have a player to send them there and then. Stewart Storey, for example, rang me up when Imran was struggling with his leg. He was desperate for someone to fill in. I mentioned Dermot Reeve and he went down and did a marvellous job for them.

Then Jamie Sykes went off to understudy John Emburey and learn his cricket with Middlesex, and Keith Meddlycote, a brilliant left-armer, joined Surrey.

You have to take your hats off to the MCC. They spend up to £50,000 a year to give these lads a chance. I don't think people know about that. And we are lucky to have companies like Barclays Bank who spend thousands of pounds every year to encourage schoolboys to play cricket.

The first year is never easy for the lads, because newcomers don't get the best opportunities. I run two teams, and the older boys usually have the places.

The purpose of being on the Lord's groundstaff is to reach Test cricket. That is the pinnacle. So after a year I may say to a lad, 'Do you think you can do it? Be honest, do you think you can make a career in first-class cricket? If not, then I would prefer, for your sake and mine, that you went off to be an accountant or something.'

My worst moments come when I see players with enormous talent not finding a county. They are the ones who horrify me. Colin Sargent is an excellent example. His talent is unreal. His batting is terrific. I've lost count of the county trials he's been on. Maybe he's a bad trialist. He went to Glamorgan and did outstandingly well, but evidently not well enough. He scored more runs than anyone else in the match, but he didn't impress.

Perhaps luck has passed him by. If forced to find an explanation, I would probably say it's his mental approach. Finding a job for someone like Colin can be hard work. If a county is not looking for that type of player, there is no way I can fix him up, and he becomes lost to the game. Cricket can be great fun, but it can be cruel, too. Colin is now my assistant and he's terrific.

When Clive Rice suddenly felt his form slipping, the first move he made to put it right was to call at Lord's and ask Gordon Jenkins to bowl to him.

Gordon who?

Jenkins – tall, brisk, proudly Welsh and creeping into his fifties. A candid man whose cricket career began and ended in the oil port of Milford Haven. In the past three to four years his name has become feared by the most famous batsmen in the world. He joined the Lord's coaching staff in 1976 and is currently manager of the superb indoor school.

But it's out in the nets that his presence is most dreaded. At the last count, it was claimed he had dismissed more Test batsmen than anyone else in the game, Dennis Lillee included. The list is long and illustrious: Clive Lloyd, Mike Brearley, Mike Gatting, Graeme Fowler . . . It goes on and on.

Gordon who?

Jenkins – the man who works the bowling machine! With a mischievous smile, Jenkins recalls some of his victims:

Clive Rice came in one morning to sort out his leg side and I bowled him twice before lunch. Tell me anyone else who's done that. He faced the machine for two and a half hours, and I pitched the ball precisely where he wanted it time and time again.

When I want to shift them, it's easy. I set the machine to 'swing' and in two balls they're gone. Even the best Test batsmen find it difficult at sixty miles an hour, though they face bowlers at ninety miles an hour on the square.

Clive Lloyd asked to face it one day, so I said, 'What speed?'

'Sixty'.

And I clean bowled him. Then I slowed it down to fifty, and when I gradually went back up to seventy, he played it easily.

As Clive left the net, Steve O'Shaughnessy was standing at the back and he called out, 'You said you could hook faster balls than that, skip!'

So Clive turned round and went back. The machine hadn't long come in from America, and wasn't fitted with a transformer to control its speed. So I turned it up to maximum, made sure I was aiming wide, and the ball shot out at 125 miles an hour. Clive didn't see it. The ball was so fast that it had hit the canvas behind the stumps and rolled back to me before Clive had lifted his bat.

Being a wise man, he didn't stay for more. He came straight out, and as he ambled past I could hear him mumbling, 'That's fast, man. That's bloody fast.'

I can also use the machine for spin, but O'Shaughnessy has put me off a bit. He charged me one day and the ball crashed under the chair on which I stand to feed the machine.

Wayne Daniel was bowling in the next net, and he stopped and came over to me and said, 'Man, if he had done that to me, the next ball I would have pinned his head against the wall.'

Ken Palmer, the umpire came in early one Saturday and played the machine beautifully. Definitely one of the best. He was dressed in his ordinary day clothes. Collar and tie, and no helmet or thigh-pad. And he played it at seventy.

When the Middlesex players come in I usually set it for Imran's type of bowling. They like to face the speed and swing. Of course, the beauty of the machine is that I can pitch the ball wherever I like. I can put down a sheet of newspaper and hit it every time. And if I want to frighten anyone, it's as easy as bowling a beamer.

And Don Wilson says of this extraordinary machine:

It's great for a player who wants to polish up a shot. It's a pity we didn't have it when Martin Crowe was here to work on his on-drive.

I also like it for showing a young batsman what a bouncer is all about, though for this exercise I always use tennis balls. Batsmen shouldn't be coached to play bouncers, but they all must know that there's a ball that can fly at their head. My advice is duck or sway. Then, as your confidence grows, to start to score runs off it.

The machine's real value is seen when county and Test players come in and use if for fifteen minutes or so at the pace they expect to face in the middle.

Great surprise, even astonishment, was expressed when Sri Lanka built up their mammoth total of 491 for seven after being put in by David Gower at Lord's on 23 August 1984. Sidath Wettimuny, all grace and charm, faced the first ball and was still there at tea on the second day. He was finally dismissed for a majestic 190, and few, if anyone, could believe it had happened.

The truth is, there were 'traitors' at work. Five of the Sri Lankan party had been hard at work at the Lord's Indoor School, and Wettimuny was one. Gordon Jenkins watched them like an owl from behind his horn-rimmed glasses. He coached, plotted and advised, and the Sri Lankans lapped up every word. Gordon Jenkins:

They asked me about the openers, Fowler and Broad. 'What shall we bowl? What line? What stump?'

'Off stump! Off stump!' I said. 'Make them play. And the same with Gower.'

'And what about Botham?'

'Pads, pads all the time.' I said. 'Don't give him width or room.'

We talked for hours. Wettimuny in particular liked to face the machine. He wanted bouncers. So I speeded it up to ninety and used tennis balls. He was hit on the head once and he didn't like it at all. I told him he could thank his lucky stars it was only a tennis ball.

On the night before the Test he asked me about the wicket. I told him it was a beauty. That it would present no problems.

During those two days of his innings, I saw him at every interval. I was always with him at lunch and tea. I met him in the pavilion and kept talking to him, kept encouraging him, kept telling him to play straight and not to gamble. At tea on the second day, I said, 'Now, come on. You must keep going.'

And he turned to me and said, 'Gordon, me mentally tired. Me gone.' He was caught behind soon after that, but it was a great knock.

Our coach Colin Sargent deserves the highest praise for the way he worked with Sidath Wettimuny. And just ten minutes after Sidath was out he telephoned Colin from the pavilion and said, 'Sorry I'm out, but why don't you come over?' And he took him up to the dressing-room, which I thought was terrific.

Then on the third day I happened to be in the pavilion again and Graeme Fowler stopped me and said, 'We've been talking. Tell me, have those Sri Lankan lads been over at the school?'

'Yes,' I said. 'And I told them how to bowl to you.'

And Graeme smiled and said, 'You bloody traitor.' He was joking of course. I am always interested in improving the standard of the game.

The moment I shall always cherish was when four of their team came into the school after the match, took off their ties and presented them to the staff. That's what's so great about cricket. You meet such nice people. The Sri Lankan lads were the most marvellous I have ever met. And all they drank was blackcurrant and lemonade – a bit different from one or two other players I could mention. So when the President of the Sri Lankan Cricket Board asked us a short time later if we would coach two of their boys for a fortnight, we practically said, 'Put them on the next plane.'

9

Schools, clubs and educating lads

Whenever England cricket slumps to a depressing new low, the inevitable question is asked about what is being done at schoolboy level to improve the standards and give fresh hope for the future.

After the catastrophic Test defeats of 1984, when only Allan Lamb, a South African, presented any consistent resistance to the West Indians, the worries surpassed just about everything that had gone on before.

Explanations and excuses, some valid, some absurd, came pouring out to soften England's lamentable performances. Yet what puzzled most critics was why England should be so desperately short of professional expertise at a time when coaching and coaching facilities, both at club level and at schools, were the best the country had ever known.

So what was wrong? Was it all the fault of bad coaching? Bad equipment? Bad selecting? Or even bad schoolmasters?

Graham Wiltshire is one of several coaches who think the problem starts at school:

They are no longer doing enough for cricket. When the bell goes now, the first people through the gates are the teachers. They don't stay behind to encourage lads in the way they did when I went to school.

In those days the little village school used to play its part in preparing young cricketers for the future. Now the equipment is often locked away in a cupboard and left to decay. It's sad.

Even worse, many schools have been closed down as education is centralised. So even if teachers are willing to stay on, the lads have to leave at four to catch the school bus. They don't fancy walking five miles, and their mums don't fancy paying out 80p for public transport.

The first item of 'equipment' in every school should be a

wall with three painted stumps for lads to bowl and throw at. Surely that's not too much to ask?

In assessing the contribution made by schools throughout cricket-crazy Somerset, Peter Robinson provides a low mark for those in charge:

The only place cricket is played to any degree for lads in this county is at a public school like Millfield. Football seems to take precedence over everything else down here.

Schools should be more competitive with their cricket. Local leagues should be organised, just as they are for football. They would bring more needle into the game. More pressure. That's what is lacking.

And more matches should be played over a full day in place of all these silly slogging games of twenty overs.

Brian Reynolds is equally despondent about the support he receives in Northamptonshire:

Schools cricket is either non-existent, or so bad in this county is at a public school like Millfield. Football seems to have taken on the responsibility of discovering the best lads and then encouraging them to take more interest in the game.

Kevin Lyons is even more forthright in his condemnation of schools cricket in England. Drawing on his experience of ten years' coaching in Cape Town and Johannesburg, he says:

Coaching facilities are far superior in South Africa. Young players shine through. They are extremely good and ambitious. It's almost a major export.

Outside the first-class game in England, the whole structure of cricket is wrong and archaic. School matches are far too short, and, because of this, proper skill levels are not being achieved. This worries me. Flaws at grassroots have a tendency to spread right through the game, even as far as the Test Match arena.

Matches played by boys of fifteen should last all day. Batsmen of this age should learn how to accumulate eighties and hundreds. And bowlers should not be handicapped by a limited number of overs. All club matches should stretch over two days and not be restricted to forty overs or a maximum of two hours for each batting side. What England needs are 'thinking' cricketers.

Club cricket in this country is light years behind South Africa. Our system is so dreary, it's no wonder we keep producing non-thinking players. That's why we are so defensive. English players have become mechanical. They lack imagination. There is not enough controlled aggression, and that depresses me.

Sport dominates life in South Africa. While a lad's away enjoying his cricket, his dad is playing golf, his mum is playing tennis, and his brother is playing squash. Sport is a family affair. Everyone takes advantage of the marvellous climate.

Phil Russell who, like Lyons, has coached in South Africa for many years, takes his own swipe at British schools, and at teachers, in particular. He protests:

Schools cricket is nowhere near what it used to be. And it will never be the same again. Teachers are motivated by money now, not prestige. They are no longer interested in doing well for their school in sports and games.

Schools in South Africa pride themselves in winning competitions. British schools don't think like that any more.

So the clubs have taken over the mantle of encouraging boys from the ages of fourteen to seventeen.

And a caustic David Gibson reckons that when it comes to cricket 'most masters know less about the game than the pupils they are teaching.' And to enforce his point, he recalls a telling incident:

I was coaching at The Oval one morning when a fifteen-year-old West Indian came in for a trial. He was big and aggressive and his first ball was a beauty. It clean bowled the batsman. Then he ran up and did the same thing again.

Of course, I was very impressed, and as I waited for him to bowl his third ball his sportsmaster came up and said, 'He hits the stumps all right, I know, but he doesn't move it a lot, does he?'

I was staggered. I muttered something under my breath and I walked away in disgust. I had never heard so much nonsense on a cricket field.

Alan Oakman sets a fine example for all coaches by the way he visits schools throughout his county during winter, providing detailed lectures and exhibitions as part of his tour.

I usually put a 10p piece on the ground and ask the young bowlers to pitch the ball on it. And if they do badly, I put 20p down. It's odd, but once they see the money, they start to take an interest.

One day a little Asian lad came in, and I said to him, 'What do you bowl, my boy?'

And he replied: 'I don't, I need the money!'

Ray East's great hobby-horse is making sure that all schoolboys wear the best protective equipment:

I preach to young lads to wear good pads. And a thigh pad. There are too many flimsy pads on the market now. They provide little or no protection, and that bothers me. One solid blow from a quick bowler and the boy is hopping all over the place.

I am a fanatic when it comes to protection, especially if it's going to help a batsman's confidence. Even to the point of wearing a helmet in the nets.

Over-bearing parents who push their children and pester coaches come in for a special roasting from Colin Page, who says:

I have lost more good cricketers through interfering parents than for any other reason. I remember one boy who made nought in our second team and when I walked round the ground I found his mother hiding behind the sight-screens, crying her eyes out.

Parents are always accusing me of having my favourites. I've lost count of the fathers I have had to turn out of dressing-rooms. I keep telling them that if they think they can coach their lads better than I can, then to do the job themselves.

What I don't like is having a flaming row with a parent in front of his lad. It can be very embarrassing for the boy. And with two people telling him what to do, it's no wonder he becomes confused. At times I've even had to order parents out of our indoor schools because they've tried to take over while I've been there.

Not all parents, thank God, are boring and a nuisance.

Many of them are good friends of mine, especially George Aslett, who has never once uttered a word of opinion or criticism in all the years that Derek has been coming to me. Bill Johnson, the father of Graham, has also been first class in that respect.

In my experience, the players who make it to the top usually have extremely understanding parents. It's the players who fall by the wayside who generally have the bad ones. Bad fathers, in particular.

In supporting Page, a worried Kevin Lyons says he has seen many good careers destroyed by over-zealous parents:

Young players must be allowed to express themselves without pressure from mothers or fathers. Too much stress can turn a lad against the game of cricket. I have seen many boys switch to something that was never their first choice – merely because they couldn't stand all the parental pressure.

Families have even broken up through it. Lads have literally left home, unable to cope with the strain of pushy mums and dads.

Though Alan Oakman is delighted to see his senior county players queuing up to practise in the nets from as early as January, he is strongly critical of the way that some of them carp about the promising youngsters who are seeking to make an impact in the game:

I tell them to stop grumbling and to think of how they were playing at that age.

Cricketers, I'm afraid, are only remembered for what they achieve after they reach the first team. Too many of them forget that they also struggled on the way up. That they had faults that needed straightening out. I keep hearing senior players saying 'Just look at that lad. Shocking! Awful!' So I turn to them and I tell them to be more tolerant. I remind them of the days when they made the very same mistakes, which usually shuts them up.

We all have to learn. We all have to gain experience. I remember Mike Smith playing at Oxford and he couldn't hit the ball off the square. And I remember Glamorgan's left-arm seamer Alan Watkins bowling Dexter through the 'gate' and saying, 'I thought he was supposed to be good.' Dexter was doing his apprenticeship. Watkins was suffering from loss of memory.

Oakman is one of those coaches who is constantly on the lookout for new players and regards no place as too obscure to throw up special talent:

Even if I am driving through the countryside I always stop to cast my eyes over the teams. I do the same in county matches. During lunch and tea I always go outside to look at the lads knocking about on the boundary edge. And if I see someone who looks promising I usually invite him along for a trial.

Good players are often there, right under our noses, waiting to be discovered. I wouldn't be doing my job properly if I didn't mingle with them. Many fine thoroughbreds have come out of a farmer's field.

Stewart Storey is highly enthusiastic about the skill and potential of young Neil Lenham, talented son of Les Lenham, former Sussex batsman and now a regional coach with the National Cricket Association:

At seventeen, Neil was the best batsman I had ever seen at that age. I am confident he will play for England before he is twenty-three. He has obviously been coached from the time he could grip a bat. And he has the right mental attitude for scoring runs. He has hit more than twenty centuries already.

What makes him really special is his willingness to listen. That is very important. If a player won't listen to his coach at that age, then he has a terrible problem. I am a great believer in speaking frankly to players who find it hard to listen. If I feel a lad isn't paying enough attention I usually say, 'If you think you know the lot, you'd better carry on in your own sweet way. You're a fool to yourself, young man.'

Of course there are certain senior professionals who think they know the lot. They won't take criticism without giving their own bit of backchat. So I say to them, 'I shall mention one or two things which you may not like because we have to sort the wheat from the chaff, but the moment you give the impression that you don't want to listen, you will get less and less advice from me.'

It is more difficult for a lad coming into county cricket now than ever before. In my time it was the same routine day in, day out. Now a batsman can play five different types of innings in a week. That is why so many technical problems occur.

In a one-day match a batsman can steer the ball without fear down to third-man and run a single. In a three-day game he'll find four slips and a gully waiting like vultures to gobble up a catch.

Opportunities come too quickly now. Twenty years ago a boy had to wait several years for his chance. Now he can come on the staff and play county cricket in his first season. There is no apprenticeship any longer.

Ken Higgs is plainly bothered that today's young cricketers don't think hard enough about the strengths and weaknesses of players in opposing teams:

When lads come to us they seem to think we are kidding them about strategy and tactics. They don't see the advantage of knowing as much as possible about the other side.

One of my first games for Lancashire was against Surrey, and the great Peter May walked to the wicket. Alan Wharton was at mid-off and he came over to me and said, 'Whatever you do, Ken, don't bowl at his middle-and-leg or he'll murder you.'

So my first ball to Peter May was bang on the off stump – and he struck it through extra-cover like a bullet from a gun. And I turned to Alan Wharton, and he said, 'Well, Ken, you're on your bloody own now.' That's the type of thing that happens. Players have to fathom it out for themselves.

It is very difficult to teach young players these days. In one week they can go from a 55-over Benson and Hedges match to a three-day game, and then to a 40-over John Player or a 60-over NatWest. On a Saturday I might go up to a batsman and tell him to keep his head down. To play a long innings. Then on the Sunday we are putting him in at number eight or nine, and there are only five balls left and we want him to hit every one of them out of the ground. Many players can't adjust to that.

Already we have a lot of excellent young batsmen coming

through and if they reach their full potential we should do well for the next ten to fifteen years. If we took Chris Balderstone out of our side, the average age would be about twenty-five, which must be good.

Hard-up Worcestershire don't even have the luxury of their own indoor nets, and admit that they rely heavily on schools and local clubs to discover and encourage young players.
Basil d'Oliveira: I would love my own indoor school. A place where I could have the key so that if a lad rang up for a trial I could invite him along and look at him in private. Hopefully it will come, but it will cost a packet.

When we want an indoor net we have to hire a sports hall at a local school. It has five nets and a first-class area for coaching, but it doesn't belong to us, and that worries me, because I am limited in what I can do. Every other county has a well-equipped indoor school.

In an ideal world I would like to invite the best lads in Worcestershire to a special net twice a week between November and April. That would be progress. That would bear fruit. But unlike the other counties we don't undertake much coaching in winter.

I know that Leicestershire and Northamptonshire often use their indoor schools as a dining-room, which is a fine way of supplementing their income.

Provided people keep pushing and pushing, I am confident we shall get our school in the end.

Proud of his club's close connection with the Nottinghamshire schools, Ken Taylor says:
I know people make a lot of noise about us and overseas players, but when the Australians came here a few years ago we had seven or eight local chaps in the side. Kevin Cooper, John Birch, Paul Johnson, Kevin Saxelby and Bruce French all came up through the schools' system.

Saxelby is a clever blighter. He has all sorts of 'O' and 'A' levels, but he doesn't like work. He prefers to enjoy himself doing the things he is good at. He likes to bat and bowl in matches, but he hates fielding, though he's much better at it now. He applies himself more. He is more mature.

He's a quick bowler when he slips himself. And intelligent

with it. He's our best John Player bowler because he's worked out how to do it. What he must understand is that he's earning his living from cricket, so he must work hard. At times he has the most horrific lapses in the field. The ball goes through his legs, and sometimes he misses it completely as it rolls along the ground. But he's a good prospect for all that.

So is Paul Johnson. He can slaughter any attack but usually gets himself out by doing something stupid. He must learn not to throw his wicket away early on.

Clive Rice and Richard Hadlee have been a big help to Kevin Cooper, who now knows what can be achieved by effort and practice and he is much more responsible because of that.

Graham Wiltshire is convinced that a lot of what a coach does to help young players often goes unnoticed:
We fight for the lads at important meetings. We push them on privately. We work hard behind the scenes, but no one gets to know. No one gets the credit.

The nicer lads hang on to every word you tell them. They lift themselves higher than if they were left alone to come on naturally. A coach helps them over the hump. A lad is usually fifteen before a county coach can look at him seriously with a view to a professional career. Boys of nine, ten and eleven might look potentially good, but a million and one things can go wrong as they grow into their teens.

The pressure of doing well in exams is greater than ever before. The only exam I ever sat was the School Certificate, which was held in the last two weeks of the summer term. On top of that, in my time in the sixth form only one boy usually went on to university. Now just about everyone goes.

These days I think most boys try their hand at every type of sport, but there comes a time when they must decide what they do best and then devote all their energy to perfecting their skill in the game they choose.

Though well-satisfied with the highly organised scouting net that Lancashire use to trawl the farthest corners of the county, John Savage still believes that more could be done at certain schools to produce young cricketers. 'Some don't even bother to play the game, which is horrifying.'
Don Bennett has every right to boast about the excellent youth

system that exists in Middlesex, where any boy worth a trial, from nine or ten upwards, is carefully assessed.

A vote of thanks is due mainly to those sympathetic clubs who stepped in during the mid-sixties and offered their facilities and time to lads left out in the cold when a number of North London schools decided to drop cricket – a sad, and mystifying move which is now being slowly and systematically rectified.

Don Bennett: We were horrified when the schools stopped playing the game, and three or four club cricketers in particular were so disappointed that they began to organise matches and practice for the boys who wanted to play.

Until that time there were barely a handful of colt sides in Middlesex, but now there are hundreds, and all playing a good standard of cricket.

Mike Gatting is one player who came up through our colts and he doesn't forget it. He is marvellous with the lads. If he carries on playing the way he is I think he will average more runs for us than any other batsman since the War.

The value of using tennis balls to coach schoolboys, and even young professionals, is hammered home by Kevin Lyons:

When teaching a lad a specific shot, say a cover-drive, I usually throw tennis balls from ten to fifteen yards. Then I test his reactions by throwing a ball that is not quite in the same spot and requires an entirely different shot. The talented lad will realise what I have done and make the right adjustment, but the average lad will continue to drive and tie himself in knots.

Whenever I work with lads of twelve to thirteen years of age, I begin by testing them for co-ordination. I throw a ball towards them and ask them to hit it on the on-side.

From the way they react I can usually tell their ball sense. Some lads are so short of co-ordination that they miss the ball entirely and continue to miss it, no matter how many times I throw it at them.

One question I am always being asked by young players is how to decide where to bat in the order. I tell them that if they are technically sound and play straight, they should bat somewhere in the middle. Say four, five, or six. From numbers three to seven, a side is looking for someone who likes to play his shots, whereas an opener's skills are very different. He needs courage and patience to face the fast bowlers.

The actual process of lifting the bat correctly is a subject on which Peter Sainsbury has positive views:

Without exception I tell our young players to take the bat back in a flat manner and not to open it up on the backswing, which is very commonly advocated, especially at schoolboy level.

The easiest thing in life is to pick the bat up straight and then bring it down straight. If a player opens it up when he is young, he has to close it at the point of contact, and that is asking too much.

Later on in his career, a player might find that 'opening up' is a natural movement, so I allow him to carry on.

What I always insist on is a firm grip with the top hand no matter whether the player lifts the bat in a flat motion or opens it up.

Remembering that Hampshire needed at least two good looks at Gordon Greenidge before he revealed his true talent, Peter Sainsbury doesn't rely on first impressions:

I look at every boy three times when they come here in droves during the winter. I don't believe any coach can judge a boy in just one evening. A lad might be nervous or unlucky on his first visit. I need time to assess them all properly.

During the summer I often nip off to a club game to watch a player, but I never let him know that I'm there. I either stay in my car or go to some far corner of the ground so as not to be noticed. Some players are easily unsettled when they know they are being watched.

As for boys, I believe they should be allowed to play at the best possible level of cricket, irrespective of their age, provided they are not out of their depth.

There is nothing wrong in a talented twelve-year-old lad playing against boys of fifteen, as long as he can cope.

What is essential is that he enjoys himself and gains some success. If he doesn't he can become bored and may give up the game.

Doug Padgett admits he can't understand where all the Yorkshire talent comes from, especially as there is far less cricket played in the schools now compared with his young days:

Despite this fall-off we still follow schools' cricket very closely. I watch many matches and we run competitions for them. Then the best players are invited to our nets. Age never enters into it. A lad might only be twelve, but if he looks good we bring him in.

For a county side we are very young. Apart from Geoff Boycott, the oldest is David Bairstow, and he's only thirty-three. Our second team finished runners-up in 1983, and the lads were only sixteen to twenty years of age. I can't remember a younger side representing Yorkshire.

People keep asking me why English cricket can't produce great fast bowlers like they do in the West Indies. Frankly I think it has a lot to do with the kids out there. All they want to do is imitate the big names – their heroes. Every lad in the West Indies wants to be a fast bowler – a Marshall or a Holding, because they don't have many great spinners to copy in the Caribbean.

A committed youth policy is also proving successful at Sussex. As many as fifteen of their twenty-one players have come through the county system, to the satisfaction of Stewart Storey:

I want us to be a Sussex side out and out. Our set-up is second to none. Any lad in this county who shows a glimmer of talent is passed on to someone inside our club for a closer look.

We are coaching boys from the age of four, and if a lad shows exceptional potential we teach him free of charge.

Boys write to me from all over Britain asking for a trial. If they are fast bowlers I see them all. If they are not, then I'm afraid their chances are limited.

Any number of boys have potential, but for one reason or another they are never seen by people who matter. Never given the opportunity to show what they can do. The wastage in this respect must be enormous.

Kent's reputation for producing home-made talent is second to none, and Colin Page is quick to give credit to the county's

*outstanding indoor facilities, and to a well-laid programme geared
to discovering good boys as early as ten:*

When I played, we had no indoor facilities. We said
goodbye in September and met up again in April. Everything
has changed now. We have four first-class indoor schools
spread right through the county.

*Thanks mainly to the Woolwich Building Society, who hand Kent
£6,500 a year to use on coaching, every schoolboy who represents
the county is given a part-sponsored course during the winter to
improve his game.*
Colin Page: For many years I have worked with the
Association of Kent Cricket Clubs, using their excellent
indoor facilities, and we've gone from strength to strength. I
am only as strong as those who do the donkey work for me. All
I do is skim the cream.

My policy is to encourage those boys who may never play
cricket for Kent but are dedicated to the game. They, too,
have every right to the best facilities. After all, they are the
people who may become some of those indispensable hard
workers you find toiling endlessly as club secretaries and
treasurers, giving up hour after hour to help others in the
game.

At all times I try not to get carried away with any success
that comes our way. I try to remember that a county side is
only as strong as the enthusiasm that exists on our village
greens.

Index

INDEX